Novalis and Mathematics

UNC | COLLEGE OF ARTS AND SCIENCES
Germanic and Slavic Languages and Literatures

From 1949 to 2004, UNC Press and the UNC Department of Germanic & Slavic Languages and Literatures published the UNC Studies in the Germanic Languages and Literatures series. Monographs, anthologies, and critical editions in the series covered an array of topics including medieval and modern literature, theater, linguistics, philology, onomastics, and the history of ideas. Through the generous support of the National Endowment for the Humanities and the Andrew W. Mellon Foundation, books in the series have been reissued in new paperback and open access digital editions. For a complete list of books visit www.uncpress.org.

Novalis and Mathematics
A Study of Friedrich von Hardenberg's Fragments on Mathematics and its Relation to Magic, Music, Religion, Philosophy, Language, and Literature

MARTIN DYCK

UNC Studies in the Germanic Languages and Literatures
Number 27

Copyright © 1960

This work is licensed under a Creative Commons CC BY-NC-ND license. To view a copy of the license, visit http://creativecommons.org/licenses.

Suggested citation: Dyck, Martin. *Novalis and Mathematics: A Study of Friedrich von Hardenberg's Fragments on Mathematics and its Relation to Magic, Music, Religion, Philosophy, Language, and Literature.* Chapel Hill: University of North Carolina Press, 1960. DOI: https://doi.org/10.5149/9781469657455_Dyck

Library of Congress Cataloging-in-Publication Data
Names: Dyck, Martin.
Title: Novalis and mathematics : A study of Friedrich von Hardenberg's fragments on mathematics and its relation to magic, music, religion, philosophy, language, and literature / by Martin Dyck.
Other titles: University of North Carolina Studies in the Germanic Languages and Literatures ; no. 27.
Description: Chapel Hill : University of North Carolina Press, [1960] Series: University of North Carolina Studies in the Germanic Languages and Literatures. | Includes bibliographical references.
Identifiers: LCCN 60062924 | ISBN 978-1-4696-5744-8 (pbk: alk. paper) | ISBN 978-1-4696-5745-5 (ebook)
Subjects: Novalis, 1772-1801. | Mathematics — History.
Classification: LCC PD25 .N6 NO. 27 | DCC 510/ .9

PREFACE

The present study grew out of my dual interest in literature and mathematics. Though literature, mainly German, is my principal field of endeavor, I have, as an adventure in thought, and in search for basic methods and principles, successfully completed a dozen advanced courses in mathematics within the Canadian honors program.

Although interest in Novalis' fragments, and in other early Romantic fragments, is growing steadily, Novalis' fragments on mathematics have, apart from Käte Hamburger's basic study, been treated in the most sciolistic manner, for two obvious reasons. First, many mathematicians who are not also historians of mathematics, limit their attention to contributions advancing the formal science of mathematics. Novalis made no such contribution. Second, many literary critics and scholars are either not qualified to deal with the subject, or are prejudiced against mathematics, which they vaguely associate with computation and technology. While mathematics is indeed highly applicable in these fields, most pure mathematicians regard this useful aspect of mathematics as an incidental and accidental feature that does not concern them, just as the literary writer would view the use of his medium of expression in, say, advertising. Mathematics, on the proper level, is a magnificent web of thought expressed in a subtle net of symbols, affording, if one is willing and able to master it, aesthetic experiences of the same order as those afforded by music and poetry, opening to the imagination vistas as bold and colorful and exciting as in the most Kafkaesque work of literature. Many prominent literary figures have been aware of the aesthetic and thought-challenging qualities of mathematics. Novalis was one of them. He devoted himself intensively to this science throughout his brief adult life. Yet critical opinion on the exact relationship of Novalis to mathematics, as much as there is of it, has fluctuated from one extreme to the other, from describing Novalis' fragments on mathematics as manifestations of a morbid mind to detecting in them an adumbration of the theory of relativity. This state of opinion, though steadily moving toward mature evaluation, demands an elucidation of the relationship of Novalis to mathematics. That is the purpose of the present study.

The first version of this study was presented in 1956 to the Graduate School of Arts and Sciences of the University of Cincinnati as a doctoral dissertation under the title "The Relation of Novalis to Mathematics." Since then I have learned a great deal more about the subject, especially from research conducted in the M.I.T. and Harvard Libraries during 1956-1958. Hand in hand with this study, a cognate monograph entitled "Goethes geistige Welt im Lichte der Mathematik" is nearing completion. Essential results of the latter were published in two American journals: "Goethe's Views on Pure Mathematics," *Germanic Review*, XXXI (1956), pp. 49-69, and "Goethe's Thought in the Light of His Pronouncements on Applied and Misapplied Mathematics," *Publications of the Modern Language Association of America*, LXXIII (1958), pp. 505-515. On the basis of these endeavors the dissertation was re-written.

I wish to express my gratitude to Professors Edwin H. Zeydel, Gottfried F. Merkel, and K. W. Maurer for continuous support, criticism, and help; to Privatdozent Dr. Alexander Peyerimhoff (Giessen), Visiting Professor of Mathematics at the University of Cincinnati, for reading the manuscript from the mathematical point of view and providing it with better formulations and various emendations; to Professor Dr. Joseph Ehrenfried Hofmann (Tübingen), noted historian of mathematics, who examined difficult fragments on mathematics by Novalis, identified them in historical contexts and offered invaluable bibliographical references; to my mathematics teachers at the University of Manitoba, in particular Professors J. W. Lawson and N. S. Mendelsohn, who graciously tolerated my "bigamous" association with literature and mathematics; to members of the mathematics staff at the University of Cincinnati and M.I.T.; to my graduate student, Mr. Emery E. George, whose critical reading of the final version of the manuscript resulted in several improvements; to my colleagues, Professors Henry W. Nordmeyer and Walter A. Reichart, to Mr. F. D. Wieck, Director of the University of Michigan Press, and to Professor Frederic E. Coenen, for their kind advice and help in the publication of the book.

I also wish to acknowledge my debt of gratitude to the Libraries of the Universities of Manitoba, Cincinnati, Harvard, and of Michigan; of the Massachusetts Institute of Technology; to the Cincinnati and New York Public Libraries; and to the Library of Congress.

Finally, I wish to thank Dean Ralph A. Sawyer and the Executive Board of the Horace H. Rackham School of Graduate Studies of the University of Michigan for a subsidy from the Publication Fund of the School, which made publication of this book possible.

May 1, 1959.   MARTIN DYCK

Department of Germanic Languages and Literatures
University of Michigan, Ann Arbor

die,
Marieche,
mine lewe fru.

Published with aid from the Publication Fund of the Horace H. Rackham School of Graduate Studies of the University of Michigan

TABLE OF CONTENTS

PREFACE	1
DEDICATION	3
CHAPTER I - INTRODUCTION	10
1. The Problem	12
2. The Sources	13
3. Critical Discussion of Previous Studies on the Subject . .	15
CHAPTER II - THE IMPACT OF MATHEMATICS ON NOVALIS	20
1. Some Aspects of the History of Mathematics in the Eighteenth Century	20
2. Novalis' Study of Mathematics and His Acquaintance with Mathematicians	25
3. Philosophical Sources for Novalis' Fragments on Mathematics	37
4. Mathematical Sources for Novalis' Fragments on Mathematics	46
CHAPTER III - NOVALIS' FRAGMENTS ON MATHEMATICS, PART ONE	52
MATHEMATICS DISCUSSED PHILOSOPHICALLY . . .	52
1. Basic Concepts	52
2. Geometry	58
3. Arithmetic and Algebra	61
4. Analysis	68
CHAPTER IV - NOVALIS' FRAGMENTS ON MATHEMATICS, PART TWO	75
MATHEMATICAL CONCEPTS PROJECTED INTO FIELDS OF KNOWLEDGE OTHER THAN THE PHYSICAL SCIENCES	75

1. Mathematics as the Ideal Science and the Basis for a
Universal Encyclopedia of Knowledge 75
2. Mathematics and Philosophy 77
3. Mathematics and Magic 79
4. Mathematics and Religion 80
5. Mathematics and Language 81
6. Mathematics and Literature 83
7. Mathematics and Music 89

SUMMARY AND CONCLUSIONS 93

BIBLIOGRAPHY 95

INDEX 104

CHAPTER I

INTRODUCTION

> Novalis, a man of the most indisputable talent, poetical and philosophical; whose opinions, extraordinary, nay altogether wild and baseless as they may often appear, are not without a strict coherence in his own mind, and will lead any other mind, that examines them faithfully, into endless considerations; opening the strangest enquiries, new truths, or new possibilities of truth, a whole unexpected world of thought, where, whether for belief or denial, the deepest questions await us (*Critical and Misc. Essays*, London, 1847, p. 5).
>
> THOMAS CARLYLE, 1827

1. THE PROBLEM

When Novalis, the German Romantic poet and philosopher, whose real name was Georg Friedrich Philipp von Hardenberg, died in 1801, not quite twenty-nine years old, there was left among his papers a large number of notes on philosophy, literature, religion, medicine, mathematics, engineering, the natural sciences, and many other branches of knowledge. These notes were either not intended for publication or were to be revised and reorganized before publication. They are usually referred to as "fragments" (*Fragmente*) or "aphorisms" (*Aphorismen*). The term fragments is preferred by those who, like the author, believe that the notes form part of a whole. The designation aphorisms is favored by those who regard the notes as spontaneous, incoherent utterances. We shall call them fragments. Research on these fragments has led scholars to the most diverse conclusions about them. Some of the fragments are lecture notes. Critics concluded that most of them are. Some fragments are excerpts from the works of contemporary philosophers and scientists, or are closely related in subject matter to such works. On that basis some critics claimed that all the fragments lack in originality and are half-digested gleanings from the works of these philosophers and scientists. These generalizations contain a grain of truth, but as they stand they are untenable because they are not borne out by facts.

The spinal cord of Novalis' fragments is mathematics. By this statement we do not mean that the fragments on mathematics constitute the largest portion, for they amount to only about five percent of the hitherto published quantity. It is the importance of these pronouncements as co-ordinates revealing the cohesion of, and permitting reference within, his thought in the kaleidoscope of his fragments, that accords them precedence over the others. During the one hundred and fifty years of Novalis research, especially during the first one hundred, it was customary to minimize the significance of these fragments. The main reasons for such treatment have been the following:

(1) Novalis scholars, who were usually not conversant with mathematics, did not know what to do with the fragments on this subject, and hence did not publish a fair amount of them in proportion to the share the fragments on mathematics occupy within the entire collection. Only the most irrational and abstruse fragments on mathematics were published by the earlier editors as elegant variations of the pronouncements of a mystical poet.

(2) Since Tieck's rhapsodical and obscuring presentation (see below) of Novalis, the latter has become so enshrouded in nebulous mysticism that it is now almost impossible to dispel the magical aura that surrounds him, and to see him as he really was. He has become the epitome of romanticism, and what seems on the surface to be more opposed to mathematics? He has been portrayed as the apostle of night and death, and who would expect such a poet to utter anything sensible on mathematics? He has been placed in the great tradition of mysticism along with Eckhart and Böhme, and what other association with mathematics could be more irksome to a mathematician?

We have set ourselves the task of examining Novalis' fragments on mathematics and elucidating every aspect of them. This task is carried out partly for the benefit of those students of Novalis who are not mathematicians but notice that Novalis wrote notes couched in mathematical terms and think that they must make sense from the strictly mathematical point of view, merely because they have been set down. The study is partly undertaken for the benefit of those professional mathematicians who may have occasion to inspect Novalis' fragments and discover that mathematical concepts are applied, or misapplied, to subject matter which is not usually treated mathematically and which does not fit into the established mathematical systems, and who therefore conclude that these fragments cannot possibly make sense. We may state from the outset that Novalis' fragments on mathematics are philosophical and not technical. From the point of view of the strict mathematician they are unrigorous and arbitrary, and contribute nothing to the technical aspects of the science of mathematics. No sooner has Novalis entered the magnificent edifice of mathematics, than he has already transgressed its boundaries into the jungle of philosophical ideas, into which no mathematician in his capacity as a mathematician will follow him for fear that he may find the ground too slippery and prove defenceless among the strange untamed animals that inhabit these dark regions.

In the present study we shall endeavor to follow the flights of Novalis' thought with due regard to the official, generally accepted results of the disciplines he enters, but, in evaluating his thought, we shall not use these official standards as measuring rods with absolute and exclusive validity. If he associates mathematics with religion, or with magic, or with any other branch of knowledge, which has not yet developed, and perhaps never will develop, into a systematic science, we shall try to find out *why* his thoughts strayed off, as it may seem, to such unusual associations of ideas, *how* such "mnemonic irrelevances" crept in, and *what* he attempted to say. It will be seen that he is exceedingly consistent within his own embryonic system of thought, although he is not bound by the shackles of any formal discipline. We shall experience the flux of ideas in an original mind, against the fixity of established facts and theories in the background. In his seemingly fantastic ideas on mathematics there will be discernible a deep insight into the nature of this science.

2. THE SOURCES

A considerable amount of Novalis' fragments has been published, bit by bit, in small doses whose composition depended on the editors' inclinations and their prescriptions for the readers. However, a large number of them, in fact the largest part, has not been published to this day.

The first edition of the works of Novalis was brought out in two volumes by Ludwig Tieck and Friedrich Schlegel in 1802, and reprinted in 1805, 1815, 1826 (in an enlarged edition), and in 1837. Volume II of this edition contains fragments. These fragments constitute only fourteen percent of those contained in the Kluckhohn-Samuel edition, the standard and, with minor exception, largest edition to date.[1] However, since the Kluckhohn-Samuel edition presents only a "limited selection" of the fragments on natural sciences and mathematics (*cf*. III, 10), because "die vollständige Veröffentlichung dieser Studien und Notizen würde aber mehrere Bände erfordern," the fragments published by Tieck and

[1] *Novalis' Schriften* (Leipzig & Berlin, 1929). In the present study, Roman and Arabic numerals in parentheses following quotations from Novalis' works, refer to volume and page, respectively, of this edition.

Schlegel in 1802 cannot amount to more than three to five percent of Novalis entire literary estate. The following passages in the Tieck-Schlegel edition (we are using the fifth, *i.e.*, slightly enlarged edition of 1837) deal with mathematics: II, 115, lines 6-7, 16-17; 119, lines 1-2 from below; 145, lines 5-14; from 145, line 20 to 149, line 2 (which includes the "hymns to mathematics," as W. Dilthey called them); 197, lines 2-4, 17; 199, lines 16-27; 200, lines 12-16; 202, lines 2-5; 250, line 14.

The bulk of this very small selection of Novalis' pronouncements on mathematics consists of "hymns to mathematics," to use Dilthey's expression, such as: "Echte Mathematik ist das eigentliche Element des Magiers," "Das höchste Leben ist Mathematik," "Reine Mathematik ist Religion," "Zur Mathematik gelangt man nur durch eine Theophanie." These few are the most enigmatical and inexplicable pronouncements of Novalis on mathematics and differ radically in content from, for example, "Mathematisches Heft" (III, 17-20), or "Arithmetica universalis" (III, 23-25), both first published in 1929. Yet for over a century of Novalis research the "hymns to mathematics" had been the basis for the evaluation of Novalis' thought on the subject, and it is not surprising that such evaluation resulted in an incomplete and distorted presentation of Novalis' views. The question naturally arises what impelled Schlegel, who selected, with the exception of those that had appeared during the poet's lifetime, the fragments from Novalis' unpublished papers for the first edition, to make such an arbitrary and non-representative selection of mathematical fragments for this edition? Schlegel's procedure is partly explained by the attitude of Tieck, his co-editor, the originator of the Novalis legend.[1] Tieck seized upon every incident in the life of Novalis that lent itself to mystification and built a legend around it. While he extolled Novalis' intellectual powers occasionally, it is clear that he did it merely to enhance him as a mystic. The kernel of the legend is, as is well known, the death of Novalis' fifteen-year old bride Sophie von Kühn on March 19, 1797, and his ensuing emotional crisis, during which he wrote that he wanted to join her in the Hereafter. Tieck writes about Sophie: "Alle diejenigen, welche diese wundersame Geliebte unseres Freundes gekannt haben, kommen darin überein, dass es keine Beschreibung ausdrücken könne, in welcher Grazie und himmlischen Anmut sich dieses überirdische Wesen bewegt... Novalis ward zum Dichter, sooft er nur von ihr sprach" (IV, 451). Further, we read in the

---

[1] See Edwin H. Zeydel, *Ludwig Tieck, the German Romanticist* (Princeton, 1935), p. 127; see also J. F. Haussmann, "German Estimates of Novalis from 1800 to 1850," *Modern Philology*, IX, p. 404, and Eduard Havenstein, *Friedrich von Hardenbergs ästhetische Anschauungen*, Palaestra, LXXXIV (Berlin, 1909), p. vii.

preface to the third (1815) edition of Novalis' works: "So kann uns sein Leben selbst mit Recht wunderbar erscheinen, und ein sonderbarer Schauer, wie bei einem Märchen, erfasst uns, wenn wir hören, dass jetzt von seinen vielen Geschwistern nur noch zwei Brüder leben" (IV, 456). It cannot be denied that Sophie's death was the deepest experience, or "Urerlebnis," in Novalis' life, nor can it be disproved that Novalis himself, under the immediate impact of her death, ascribed supernatural powers to her and fancied to communicate with her spirit. However, a line must be drawn between a temperate critical assessment of a poet with mystical propensities and a mystical presentation of mysticism, *i.e.*, mysticism to the second degree, which obscures rather than illuminates the thought of a poet. Tieck disregards this line. His impressions about "überirdisches Wesen," "sonderbarer Schauer," *etc.*, have had such mythopoeic effect that a sober approach to Novalis was for a long time out of the question.

In selecting the fragments for publication, Schlegel, no doubt in close consultation with Tieck, sought to emphasize those pronouncements which at first glance seem paradoxical and absurd, because they have the greatest semblance of originality. It is understandable that under such conditions the imperspicuous hymns to mathematics were selected, and that the more lucid pronouncements on mathematics did not have much of a chance to be included. We also know about Friedrich Schlegel's mastery in concocting fragments. He is said to have gone over Novalis' or his own notes on sundry subjects and to have selected some striking sentences and deliberately obscured them by dissolving them from their contexts (see editor's preface, *Novalis Schriften*, ed. J. Minor, I, xlii).

In 1846 Tieck and Eduard von Bülow published a third volume of Novalis' writings. This volume contains a selection of Novalis' diaries, letters, poems, fragments, and a biography by Tieck. It brought the amount of Novalis' published fragments to 32% of the fragments contained in the Kluckhohn-Samuel edition, which again constitutes a much smaller portion of the entire literary estate of Novalis. The following fragments contained in Volume III deal with mathematics: pp. 61, line 6; 121, lines 14-20; 184, lines 1-19, line 22; 245, lines 5-14; 246, lines 10-26; 284, lines 7-12; 296, lines 10-15; 313, line 23. Although some of these observations on mathematics are important, one gets the impression that they were included by chance rather than by design. Tieck's preface tends to mystify rather than clarify the meaning of the fragments. His concluding words are the following: "Mit Wehmut und nicht ohne eine Art von Andacht übergebe ich nach fast fünfzig Jahren diese Reliquien eines edlen und grossen Geistes den Freunden der echten Mystik" (*Novalis Schriften*, ed. Tieck & Bülow, Berlin, 1846, p. vi).

Such a preface is not conducive to an objective evaluation of Novalis' observations on mathematics. Bülow tells us in the preface to this volume that he did most of the work in preparing it, but the selection indicates that he hardly deviated from the principles laid down by Tieck.

The next important edition of Novalis' works is the one published by Ernst Heilborn in 1901.[1] He made an attempt to arrange the fragments chronologically, in the hope that such an arrangement would clarify those of the fragments which seemed contradictory to him. To Heilborn Novalis' thought is haphazard: "Novalis dachte in Gedankensprüngen: um so interessanter, diese lockeren und oft ganz zufälligen Ideenassoziationen zu verfolgen" (*Ibid.*, I. Teil, x). His edition contains 62% of the amount of the fragments in the Kluckhohn-Samuel edition. While there is some increase in the number of fragments relating to mathematics, Heilborn did not publish the following manuscripts with mathematical content. The listing here includes brief descriptions of the contents of the manuscripts, as given by Heilborn in his edition of Novalis' works (II. Teil, 2. Hälfte, pp. 682ff.):

"Die in den Text nicht aufgenommenen Manuskripte.

Mz. 1 Bl. folio, bez. Nr. XLII (1 u. 2) "Meine Bemerkungen." Über Zählen und Rechnen."Rechnen und Denken ist eins." Über mathematisches Genie. "Genie ist das synthesierende Prinzip; das moralisierende, transsubstantiierende Prinzip."

Mk. 4 Bl. quart, bez. Nr. LII (1-4). "Mathematisches Heft." Zahlensystem ist Muster eines Sprachzeichensystems. Antithetischer (todter) und synthetischer (lebendiger) Zustand jeder Substanz. Organisches Leben ist Produkt beider. Die Natur als Mathematiker. Über Friktion.

Ta "Logologische Fragmente." –

Tb folio 15. Auszug aus astronomischen Werken.

Of. Kategorien.... – Über die Mathematik...

Oh (pag. 56-59 der Handschrift O). Über Wesen und Eigenschaft. "Gott und Welt, wie Natur und Geist." Über den Begriff des Zählens...

Pc (pag. 1 und 2 der Handschrift P). Auszüge aus Gehler über Unendlichkeitsrechnung; aus Hemsterhuis...

---

[1] *Novalis' Schriften*. Kritische Neuausgabe auf Grund des handschriftlichen Nachlasses von Ernst Heilborn, 3 Teile (Berlin, 1901). This edition was severely criticized by J. Minor, *Anzeiger für deutsches Altertum*, XXVIII, 82ff., Oskar Walzel, *Euphorion*, IX, 456ff., and A. H. von Hugenstein, *Euphorion*, XIII, 79ff., 515ff. Despite its philological shortcomings, and partly because of them, this edition is important as it served as a basis for much scholarly work. Other less important editions prior to Heilborn's were: *Werke*, ed. J. Dohmke (Leipzig, 1892), *Schriften*, ed. Carl Meissner (Leipzig, 1898).

Pd (pag. 4-9 der Handschrift P). Mathematisches. Über unendliche Reihen, exponentielle Grössen, Differentialcalcül. Die Theorie des Infinitesimalcalcüls. Unterschied der Methode zwischen gemeiner und höherer Mathematik. Algebra und Analysis. Die verschiedenen Sätze der Mathematik (Axiom, Postulat, Theorem usw.) Über die Theoreme.
– Über Mathematik und Philosophie. Worte und Figuren bestimmen sich in beständigem Wechsel. Figurenworte. – Axiome und Postulate der Arithmetik.

Pe (pag. 12 der Handschrift P). Die Frage nach der Weltsubstanz, eine antinomische..."

"Salinenschriften.

10. 2 Bl. folio. Mathematische Arbeiten (zur geom. Progression).

11. 2 Bl. folio. Mathematische Arbeiten (Logarythmen, Wurzeln, arithmetische Progressionen).

12. 2 Bl. folio. Mathematische Arbeiten (Zur elementaren Geometrie. "Kästners Analysis.")

23. 2 Bl. folio. Notizen über vorzunehmende Arbeiten, darunter Mathematik doppelt unterstrichen.

24. 4 Bl. quart. "Principes pour la résolution des triangles rectangles." – "Trigonométrie Sphérique."

31. 1 Bl. folio. Kosten- und Gewinnberechnung a) der Freibergischen Schmelzarbeiten b) der Amalgamirarbeiten an der Halsbrücke."

In 1907 Jakob Minor published an edition of Novalis' works in four volumes (*Novalis Schriften*, Jena, 1907). In addition to the fragments published in the Tieck-Schlegel-Bülow edition, Minor included in his edition the fragments published for the first time in the Heilborn edition. The number of fragments published by Minor constitutes 59% of the amount contained in the Kluckhohn edition. The passages referring to mathematics are found on the following pages:
Vol. II, pp. 18, 88, 107, 172, 178, 183, 208, 251, 253f., 259, 262-269, 286.
Vol. III, pp. 9, 19, 36, 38, 42, 82f., 95, 104; the following were reprinted from the Heilborn edition: 167, 173, 181, 206, 213, 249f., 268, 277, 285, 291, 294f., 297, 318, 325, 333ff., 339f., 342, 347, 373.
Vol. IV, pp. 246, 255.
The standard and essentially most complete edition of Novalis' writings was published by Kluckhohn and Samuel in 1929.[1] The

---

[1] See footnote 1. E. Kamnitzer in his edition of the *Fragmente* (Dresden, 1929), and E. Wasmuth in his editions of *Briefe und Werke* (Berlin, 1943), and *Werke, Briefe, Dokumente* (Heidelberg, 1954ff.) have added a few odd fragments to the collection contained in the Kluckhohn-Samuel edition. Carl Seelig's edition, *Novalis, Gesammelte Werke*, 5 vol.s (Herrliberg-Zürich, 1945f.), brings no new material. During the interval between Minor's (1907) and the Kluckhohn-Samuel (1929) editions there appeared *Werke*, ed. H. Friedmann (Berlin, 1913) and *Sämtliche Werke*, ed. E. Kamnitzer (Munich, 1924), neither of which improved on Minor.

edition includes previously published material and a number of unpublished writings. The following fragments on mathematics were published here for the first time (cf. list III, 399-402):

III, 17, line 17 to III, 20, line 7 Hs. MLII "Mathematisches Heft"
III, 23, lines 10-23 Aus Hs. MXLVIII "Algemeine Naturlehre oder algebraische Physik."
III, 23, lines 24-26 Aus MXLVI "Physikalische Fragmente."
III, 23, line 27 to III, 25 Hs. MXLII "Arithmetica Universalis."
III, 52, lines 1-3 Hs. MXL
II, 106, lines 8-9 Hs. ohne Signatur. Überschrift "Hauptregel," Blatt 1-4
II, 122, lines 21-24 Hs. K Blatt 49-52
II, 127 Hs. "Hauptregel" Blatt 5-14
II, 141, lines 7, 15-19 Hs. O 113-116
II, 160, lines 13 through bottom of page Hs. K44
II, 188, line 27 Hs. N 1-4 "Grundsätze der Algebra angewandt auf Metaphysik."
II, 214, lines 4-6 Hs. O 95-102
II, 249, line 10 Hs. O 23-32 "Algeber - Schicksal. Rhapsodik."
II, 252 Hs. O 23-32, 37-40 "Geometrie"
II, 253, lines 24-36 Hs. M xxxiv, Blatt 3, 4
II, 260, line 23 Hs. Beilage zu N 1
II, 264, lines 8-9 Hs. O 84-89
II, 267, lines 2-3 Hs. O 33-36
II, 269; 280, lines 15-16 Hs. K 15, 16
II, 284-286 Hs P 1, 2 (Auszüge aus Gehler, Hemsterhuis, Dumas)
II, 289 Hs. MV (Auszüge aus Hemsterhuis über Mathematik und Wissenschaft)
II, 304, line 8 Hs. D 1, 2

Two publications by Richard Samuel inform us best about the large number of hitherto unpublished fragments and other materials of the literary estate of Novalis: *Novalis* (F. v. *Hardenberg*). *Der handschriftliche Nachlass des Dichters. Versteigerungskatalog* (Berlin, 1930) and "Zur Geschichte des Nachlasses Friedrich von Hardenbergs (Novalis)," *Jahrbuch der deutschen Schillergesellschaft*, ed. F. Martini, H. Stubenrauch, and B. Zeller (Stuttgart, 1958), II, 301-347. The fate of the largest portion of unpublished materials that concern us here is described by Samuel on p. 344 of the latter publication: "Am Ende der zwanziger Jahre dieses Jahrhunderts sah sich die Familie Hardenberg genötigt, den in Oberwiederstedt verbliebenen Nachlass abzustossen. Verhandlungen, den Gesamtbestand durch amtliche Stellen, z.B. das damalige Reichsarchiv in Potsdam, zu erwerben, scheiterten an der Beschaffung der notwendigen Mittel.

So wurde am 20. Dezember 1930 der grösste Teil des Nachlasses, der durch den Verfasser katalogisiert wurde, versteigert. Der Hauptkäufer war der Handschriftensammler und Verleger Herr Salman Schocken, der nach 1933 Deutschland verliess. In seinem Besitz sind die wichtigsten Tagebücher und die Hauptmassen der Fragmenthandschriften." I was unable to obtain photostats of hitherto unpublished fragments in this collection.

3. CRITICAL DISCUSSION OF PREVIOUS STUDIES ON THE SUBJECT

The only previous study exclusively devoted to Novalis' relation to mathematics is Käte Hamburger's article "Novalis und die Mathematik, eine Studie zur Erkenntnistheorie der Romantik," *Romantik-Forschungen. Deutsche Vierteljahrsschrift für Literaturwissenschaft und Geistesgeschichte.* Buchreihe. 16. Band (Halle, 1929), pp. 115-184. Other authors merely offer incidental comments on this problem within the framework of studies devoted to more general subjects. In our discussion, we shall proceed chronologically.

It will be convenient for the present purpose to divide the century and a half of research on Novalis since his death into three periods:

(1) The first period, 1802 to 1901, during which the Tieck-Schlegel-Bülow editions of Novalis' works, or reprints of them, were used;

(2) The second period, 1901 to 1929, during which the Heilborn and Minor editions, and reprints from them and from the editions of the first period, were used;

(3) The third period, 1929 to the present, during which the Kluckhohn-Samuel edition was and is standard.

(4) A fourth period will set in with the publication of the numerous unpublished fragments that are presently practically inaccessible to scholars.

During the first period of Novalis research the few arbitrarily chosen observations on mathematics and related fields available to scholars were regarded as intentionally mystical and were read for their aesthetic value rather than consistent meaningfulness. An exception to this general attitude was Adam Müller's conviction in his *Vorlesungen über die deutsche Wissenschaft und Literatur* (1807), p. 73, that Novalis was an ideal intermediary between scientific endeavors in Germany and the other countries (see J. H. Haussmann, *Mod. Philol.*, IX, 6).

Wilhelm Dilthey,[1] who, again, was acquainted only with the few

---

[1] "Novalis," *Das Erlebnis und die Dichtung*, 10th ed. (Leipzig & Berlin, 1929). First book edition, 1905. Article first appeared in *Preussische Jahrbücher*, 1865.

fragments on mathematics selected by non-mathematicians for their literary value alone, does not attach any significance to Novalis' thought on natural philosophy and science. "Die Hymnen auf die Mathematik sind schliesslich unfruchtbar. Ja Novalis spielt mit dem mystischen Begriff einer echten Mathematik, die im Morgenlande zu Hause sei, in Europa aber zur blossen Technik ausgeartet sei" (p. 304). He thus selects one of the most difficult passages and bases such a strong generalization on it. In his notes to the 1905 and subsequent book editions of his essay on Novalis, Dilthey admits that in 1865, when he wrote the essay, the only sources at his disposal had been the Tieck-Schlegel-Bülow editions of Novalis' works, *i.e.*, that he was acquainted with fewer than 10% of Novalis' fragments on mathematics, which, moreover, were the most difficult ones. However, despite his acquaintance with the contents of the Heilborn edition, he maintains his earlier stand in the evaluation of the fragments. He draws support for his claim from Olshausen's study on Novalis' relation to the natural sciences in which the author, not unlike Dilthey, perceives in Novalis' fragments on science "the sporadic volatility of a morbid mind" and becomes convinced that Novalis was not destined to be a philosopher or scientist. (*Friedrich von Hardenbergs Beziehungen zur Naturwissenschaft seiner Zeit*, Diss. Leipzig, 1905, p. 70).

Rudolf Haym's remarks on Novalis' fragments on mathematics are biased and exaggerated (*Die romantische Schule*. 4th ed., Berlin, 1920, first publ. 1870). He does not think much of Novalis' originality as a philosopher and therefore judges Novalis' thought by the measure of its coincidence or deviation from Kant's and Fichte's systems. Noting that, on one occasion, Novalis had expressly voiced his adherence to Kant's "Kritizismus," Haym then finds in Novalis' fragments "ein ziemlich laxer Kritizismus, und in der Tat: auch da, wo er auf die einfachsten und bewiesensten Grundlagen des Kritizismus zurückgeht, überspannt er dieselben sofort zum Überspringen durch die Intensität seines Enthusiasmus" (p. 418). One such allegedly infallible basic assumption of Kant's philosophy is that the laws of mathematics are the laws of our minds, and that as such they have absolute validity and applicability in the realm of "äussere Erscheinungen," because these, in turn, are known to us only as they impinge on our minds. This view has been discarded by mathematicians long ago (see, for example, M. Kline, *Mathematics in Western Culture*, New York, 1953, p. 251), but to Haym it was one of the "bewiesenste Grundlagen," an infallible truth by which he measured Novalis' thought. Haym further simply accords validity to those of Novalis' fragments which agree with Kant (p. 418), and dismisses those in opposition to Kant as nonsense: "Novalis wird über jener Kantschen Lehre zum Zungenredner"

(p. 418). He continues: "Über der Wahrnehmung jedoch, dass die Mathematik in der Musik 'als Offenbarung, als schaffender Idealismus' erscheine, kommt ihm alsbald alle Besonnenheit abhanden. Echte Mathematik wird nun für 'das eigentliche Element des Magiers' erklärt, die Mathematiker heissen ihm die einzig Glücklichen, das Leben der Götter soll Mathematik, reine Mathematik soll Religion sein, und was der wunderlichen Behauptungen mehr sind" (p. 419). It is evident that Haym was the victim of the Tieck-Schlegel-Bülow non-representative selections of Novalis' fragments, and that he knew little about the problems of the relation of mathematics to other fields of Novalis' time.

Ricarda Huch, in her treatment of Novalis' relation to mathematics in her work *Die Romantik* (Vol. I, *Blütezeit der Romantik*, Vol. II, *Ausbreitung und Verfall der Romantik*, 14th ed., Leipzig, 1924, first publ. in 1899), concentrates, like Dilthey and Haym, on Novalis' hymns to mathematics. "Nicht nur, dass er mit Eifer Mathematik studierte, er poetisierte sie wie alles, womit er sich beschäftigte, durchdrang sie mit seiner lebendig warmen Seele; man lese nur seine Hymnen an die Mathematik" (II, 68-69). Like Dilthey and Haym, she selects the most inscrutable observations of Novalis on mathematics, mainly because they were the only fragments accessible. Hence she fails to recognize Novalis' consistent effort to explore mathematics as a foundation for an all-inclusive system of thought. However, she makes a valuable contribution to our problem with her discussion of Wilhelm Butte's *Grundlinien einer Arithmetik des menschlichen Lebens* (Landshut, 1811) and Giovanni Malfatti's *Studien über Anarchie und Hierarchie des Wissens* (Leipzig, 1845), in which the authors deal with the Romantic conception of number. Butte held that mathematical numbers were dead shadows of the eternal, living numbers which originally had physical and philosophical connotations. Fragments of the ancient conception of numbers, Butte reminds us, came down to us through Pythagoras. Butte believed that the time of the revival of the original meaning of numbers was at hand, and that Novalis pointed in this direction. Then Huch discusses the mystical connotations of various numbers, in connection with Novalis' interpretations of 0, 1, and infinity.

Ernst Heilborn spent two years exploring the literary estate of Novalis at Oberwiederstedt. Yet in the chapter "Die Welt der Fragmente" of his book *Novalis der Romantiker* (Berlin, 1901), pp. 149-171, he fails to mention mathematics. Surely he must have had the numerous fragments on mathematics in his hands. However, he found it more convenient not to deal with them.

Egon Friedell's study *Novalis als Philosoph* (Munich, 1904) marks the beginning of the second period of Novalis research. It is characterized by a greater appreciation of, and a steadily increasing insight into, the fragments, coupled with the realization of the importance of mathematics to Novalis. Although he still describes the fragments in the hasty manner of his predecessors as "bunt aneinandergereihte Gedanken," he assures us, somewhat exaggeratedly, that truth is revealed to us through the intellect rather than through brooding fancy or wayward imagination (pp. 24, 44). Friedell is aware that Novalis regarded mathematics as the ideal of all knowledge. However, he concludes his comments on Novalis' relation to mathematics with the general statement that Novalis etherealizes and romanticizes the essence of mathematics.

A year before Friedell's book appeared, E. Spenlé had presented a doctoral dissertation on Novalis at the Sorbonne: *Novalis, essai sur l'idéalisme romantique en Allemagne* (Paris, 1903). He writes about Novalis' relation to mathematics: "L'univers se présente à lui comme une vaste équation algébrique. Il s'agit, par une réduction graduelle, de déterminer les termes inconnus en fonction des termes connus. Mais comment formuler dés à présent ces termes inconnus? Le philosophe inventera un système de notations tout-à-fait arbitraire, tiré uniquement des profondeurs de son esprit, qu'il substituera audacieusement à la réalité empirique, de même que l'algébriste désigne des grandeurs inconnues par des lettres arbitrairement choisies" (p. 139f.). "Ce qu'il s'agit de découvrir c'est donc une mathématique *dynamique* universelle où les Nombres seraient eux-mêmes des pensées actives. Cette mathématique nouvelle Novalis crut la trouver dans Fichte" (p. 142). In his few comments on Novalis and mathematics, Spenlé oversimplifies our problem, but nonetheless appreciates these fragments in the proper context and perspective.

Heinrich Simon is the first to explore the symbolic significance of mathematics to Novalis and its relation to magic idealism in his study *Der magische Idealismus* (Heidelberg, 1906), p. 24. Eduard Havenstein in his presentation of "Friedrich von Hardenbergs ästhetische Anschauungen," *Palaestra* (Berlin, 1909), LXXXIV, pp. 1-30, takes great pains to show that the Romanticists, including Novalis, suffered from a weakness of will and intellect (p. 24), that Novalis had read Kant very superficially and had not read much generally (p. 29), and that he never was seriously concerned with philosophy (p. 30). But then he admits: "...muss jedoch gleich gestehen, dass ich alles das, was ausschliesslich fachmännisch über Mathematik, Physik, Chemie etc. handelt, von meinen Untersuchungen ausgeschlossen und (nach der bisherigen Ordnung) in einer mit M bezeichneten Mappe vereinigt habe; denn erstens bin ich diesen naturwissenschaftlichen Problemen nicht gewachsen, und zweitens glaube ich nicht, dass sie zur Erkenntnis des tiefsten und innerlichsten Novalis etwas Wesentliches beitragen" (p. 3). Havenstein's attitude is characteristic. First he admits that he is unable to deal with, and hence also unable to judge, Novalis' writings on natural science and mathematics, and then he volunteers the remark that it would be of little use anyhow to our knowledge of "des tiefsten und innerlichsten Novalis." Thus, in Havenstein's own narrow mental domain there is no room for the comprehension of the grandeur and universality of Novalis' thought.

Karl Theodor Bluth's Jena dissertation *Philosophische Probleme in den Aphorismen Hardenbergs* (Jena, 1914) devotes much of its third chapter to Novalis' fragments on mathematics (pp. 26-40). Bluth is fully aware of the importance of these fragments within Novalis' thought, "offenbart sich doch in solcher Auffassung der Mathematik die ganze Tiefe von Hardenbergs philosophischem Denken. Fast erleben wir den Eindruck, als ob in diesen Problemen sein Geist das Höchste und gleichsam Unerhörteste erreichen durfte. Mehr geahnt, mehr angedeutet als scharf und offen gesichtet" (p. 27). His discussion revolves about three aspects of Novalis' mathematical thought: mathematics as rhythm, as a free creation, and as a synthetizing transcendental construction. He considers Novalis' associations of the first aspect with music, of the second with poetry, and of the third with the magical "Weltanschauung." Bluth also recognizes Novalis' conception of the second aspect, *i.e.*, of mathematics and poetry as free creations, as the basis for the latter's magical world view. "Die Behauptung, dass die transzendentale Einbildungskraft mit der produktiven Einbildungskraft des Dichters identisch wäre, weil sie eben beide in der Mathematik ihr Wesen hätten, bildet die Grundlage von Hardenbergs Weltanschauung" (p. 35). Bluth's claim that Novalis abandoned mathematics during the decisive years of his life is untenable. His evidence is discussed elsewhere in this book.

Ludwig Kleeberg ("Studien zu Novalis," *Euphorion*, XXIII, 1921, pp. 635ff.) discovers a close relation of Novalis' fragments on the magic of numbers to similar observations in Volume 4 of Karl von Eckartshausen's *Aufschlüsse zur Magie aus geprüften Erfahrungen über verborgene philosophische Wissenschaften und entdeckte Geheimnisse der Natur* (Munich, 1788-1791), 4 vols. Like Novalis, Eckartshausen held that mathematics was the most sublime science; that it should be the basis of all other sciences; that magic and mathematics are interrelated. Kleeberg points out that a concordance of similar mathematical passages in the works of the two authors could be set up.

F. Imle in her study *Novalis: seine philosophische Weltanschauung* (Paderborn, 1928), pp. 41-42, is anxious not to underestimate the significance of Novalis' fragments on mathematics. She states that Novalis failed in his attempt to increase the number of categories, or to reduce them to a single "Urkategorie," or to a single psychic function. However, in the process of searching for such a reduction of the categories, Novalis gained important insights into mathematics: "Hierher gehört, was Novalis über die methodische Bedeutung der Mathematik und ferner über die erkenntnisbildende Tätigkeit der Phantasie sagt. Beides ist auf den ersten Blick so übertrieben, dass der wissenschaftliche Kritiker nur zur Ablehnung gestimmt wird, hat aber bei gründlicherer Betrachtung... immerhin den Wert einer beachtenswerten Abschleifung der Kanten des Kantischen Nur-Rationalismus" (p. 41). Imle recognizes that to Novalis mathematics was a universal tool of all arts and sciences, "Welterkenntnisschlüssel." She points out that to Novalis mathematics is the "Ur- und Höchstform alles Denkens." However, like most previous critics of Novalis' relation to mathematics, Imle merely rephrases some of the poet's most striking observations on mathematics and attaches value judgments to them, yet within her treatment of Novalis' philosophy her comments on mathematics are incidental.

When through the publication of the Kluckhohn-Samuel edition of Novalis' works in 1929 much additional material became available, scholars suddenly realized how Novalis had been misjudged in previous evaluations of his fragments. Hence they set out to explore them anew. This third stage of Novalis research is marked by the first systematic investigation of the fragments, and also the first realization of the significance of mathematics in Novalis' thought.

Käte Hamburger undertakes the first and to date only study of the relation of Novalis to mathematics (see above). She proposes to show that while Novalis was not a creative mathematician, he nevertheless grasped the theoretical foundations of mathematics, mostly intuitively, "aber mit einem geradezu erstaunlichen logischen Instinkt" (p. 118). She further states: "Wir finden bei Novalis eine geradezu philosophische Bemühung um die Grundlagen der von Leibniz und Newton begründeten neueren Mathematik" (p. 118). Hamburger then sets out to show the symbolical meaning of mathematics in Novalis' Romantic philosophy of life. The hymns to mathematics are explained in conjunction with Novalis' magic idealism, Kant's concept of synthesis and synthetic judgments, and Ernst Cassirer's ideas on the affinities between magic and scientific thought, as set forth in *Philosophie der symbolischen Formen*; II. Teil, *Das mythische Denken* (Berlin, 1926), pp. 31ff. She interprets the transition from Kant's critical idealism to Novalis' magic idealism in such a manner "dass der auf die Spitze getriebene kritische Idealismus sozusagen umschlägt in ein vorwissenschaftliches, magisches Verhalten der Seele" (p. 119).

Hamburger points out the agreement between Novalis' conception of the independence of mathematics from extra-mathematical reality and similar views among pure mathematicians. According to Hamburger, the central concern in Novalis' meditations on mathematics is his preoccupation with the logical and epistemological foundations of infinitesimal calculus. Here she points out parallels in the thought of Novalis and that of such modern philosophers as Cohen, Natorp, Husserl, and B. Russell (p. 129). In connection with calculus, and in the light of its interpretations by the above-mentioned authors, especially Cassirer (in particular, *Substanz- und Funktionsbegriff*, 2nd ed., Berlin, 1923) and Natorp (*Die logischen Grundlagen der exakten Wissenschaften*, Leipzig, 1910), Hamburger deals with Novalis' conception of function, continuity, and infinity, but her discussion is somewhat removed from the more strictly mathematical framework for these concepts. Function, with its implications of flux, change, and growth, is a concept that must of necessity appeal to Novalis, the Romanticist. "Er ringt geradezu um den Begriff der Funktion, er spürt, dass das eigentliche 'Sein' nicht durch den Substanzbegriff einer dogmatischen Ontologie, sondern vielmehr durch den Relationscharakter der Funktion charakterisiert werden muss" (p. 135). The mathematical concept of infinity was particularly attractive to Novalis. Hamburger explains that whereas Friedrich Schlegel, Hölderlin, Tieck, and Schleiermacher mused over infinity in nature and in the universe as a postulate of metaphysics, Novalis sought to comprehend the methodical significance of infinity (p. 139). Hamburger then proceeds to explore Novalis' views on the crucial mathematical concept of continuity: "Der Gedanke der Kontinuität als Ursprungseinheit, d.h. als zugrundeliegende Allheit war also für Novalis – mit genauer mathematischer Richtigkeit – der letzte Grund, durch den die Infinitesimalrechnung sich legitimiert" (p. 165). The concept of continuity is significant in the philosophy of Leibniz, not only in his calculus, but also in his other writings. It was also of importance to Goethe, who regarded continuity as one of the characteristics of mathematics, especially mathematical method, which could be profitably employed also by the non-mathematician. Hamburger summarizes: "Wir haben aufgezeigt, wie durch das Rüstzeug der mathematischen Wissenschaft der Kontinuitätsgedanke bei Novalis aus der mystischen Intuition sich erhob in die Sphäre begrifflicher Klarheit" (p. 165).

In Novalis' reflections on time and space Hamburger detects an adumbration of the subsequent development of non-Euclidean geometry and even of Einstein's theory of relativity. She quotes Novalis' fragments "Raum und Zeit entstehen zugleich und sind wohl eins, wie Subjekt und Objekt. Raum ist beharrliche Zeit,

Zeit ist fliessender Raum..." (III, 156) and "Jeder Körper hat seine Zeit – jede Zeit hat ihren Körper" (III, 254) and points to the abandonment of the concept of absolute time and space in the four-dimensional continuum of the theory of relativity. Lest someone draw hasty conclusions about Novalis' prophetic instinct, she cautions: "Wir dürfen aus den abgebrochenen Aussprüchen des Novalis keine zu grosse Meinung über eine vorahnende Erkenntnis der modernen Relativitätstheorie bei ihm gewinnen; sie sollen nur erweisen, dass gerade der Romantik, als deren konzentriertester Ausdruck die Persönlichkeit des Novalis gelten kann, die kühnsten Kombinationen des Gedankens, ohne die der Fortgang nicht möglich wäre, besonders nahe lagen und dass sie vorzüglich den Novalis auf Ziele wiesen, die in der Tat das folgende Jahrhundert realisiert hat" (p. 184).

To Hamburger goes the credit of having made the first investigation devoted exclusively to Novalis' relation to mathematics. She deals at some length with his conception of function, continuity, infinity, time and space. However, in dealing with these concepts, she is unduly influenced by the philosophical distinctions of the Neo-Kantian school and hesitates to explore them from the more strictly mathematical point of view. She does not adequately represent the context of Novalis' fragments in the historical setting of Novalis' time. She does not, or does only insufficiently, deal with Novalis' pronouncements on definition, axiom, theorem, proof, and many other mathematical concepts which Novalis discusses, and which need elucidation. Nor does she deal with the relation of mathematics to religion, language, literature, and music.

Walter Silz in his study *Early German Romanticism* (Cambridge, Mass., 1929) is one of the first critics to note the fact that the early German Romanticists were "men of intellect, of supreme intelligence and extraordinary analytical power" (p. 11). He fails "to gain from the perusal of Novalis' writings the impression of formlessness, haziness, and confusion, which is alleged to be so typical of Romantic literature. In his fragments and letters one finds lucidity and reason, and not only the flash, but the steady glow of intellect" (p. 133). He states that Novalis was well versed in mathematics (p. 134). However, he does not deal with this subject, because it is outside the scope of the task that he has set himself, *viz.*, H. Kleist's position in early German Romanticism.

In his book *Unendliche Sphäre und Allmittelpunkt. Beiträge zur Genealogie der mathematischen Mystik* (Halle, 1937), Dietrich Mahnke states that Novalis subdivided his "mystische Mathematik" into two main branches: "Magie der Zahlen" and "mystische Geometrie" (see Novalis' fragments, II, 333; III, 18, 337, 248). In the latter branch, Mahnke investigates Novalis' conception of an important dyad in the history of ideas, infinite sphere and center of the universe, tracing this dyad through the Middle Ages to Plotinus, Plato, and the Pythagoreans.

Lydia Elisabeth Wagner attempts "a full presentation of Novalis' relation to all the science of his time throughout his brief life, excepting mathematics, which has been fully covered by Käte Hamburger" in her dissertation *The Scientific Interest of Friedrich von Hardenberg (Novalis)* (Ann Arbor, Michigan, 1937). This latter statement is false. Hamburger, as we stated above, selects only a few aspects of Novalis' relation to mathematics and hardly deals, for example, with the relation of Novalis' fragments on mathematics to his time. Such comments by Wagner that Novalis carried his train of thought in certain mathematical fragments "too far" (p. 158), are of little value in the elucidation of Novalis' views on mathematics. The formulation of her dissertation is much too broad. Numerous special fields of science in the conception of Novalis need to be explored in detailed ground work, before "a full presentation of Novalis' relation to all the science of his time" can be undertaken.

In her book *Die Fragmente des Novalis* (Basel, 1939), Anni Carlsson fails to recognize the fundamental importance of mathematics in Novalis' thought, although she remarks that Novalis' fragments on mathematics have frequently been considered from too narrow a point of view (p. 184). She deals with mathematics only in a one-page subsection "Magie und Mathematik" (p. 26) and the three-page section "Die Produkte des freien Denkens und der freien Einbildungskraft: Mathematik und Dichtung" (pp. 183-185). She essentially ignores those of Novalis' fragments on mathematics and philosophy that were first published by Kluckhohn and Samuel in 1929.

In 1941 Alexander Gode- von Aesch published his Columbia University dissertation *Natural Science in German Romanticism* (New York, 1941). In relating the concept of infinity to the historical mathematical contexts, he presents some facts from the history of mathematics, but does not enter into mathematical detail. Instead of evading the issue, as L. E. Wagner did, he frankly admits: "The interpretation of this aspect of our problem must be left to a competent mathematician" (p. 136). Otherwise his treatment of Novalis and mathematics is limited to the remark that Novalis imparts metaphysical validity to his metaphor "through his peculiar philosophy of mathematics" (p. 180).

Louis Locher-Ernst quotes some of Novalis' hymns to mathematics in his discussion of the relation of mathematics to religion and music in the collection of papers entitled *Mathematik als Vor-*

schule zur Geist-Erkenntnis (Zurich & Kreuzlingen, 1944), pp. 11, 12, 15, 16, 24.

Maurice Besset throws some light on the interrelations of mathematics and mysticism in his study *Novalis et la pensée mystique* (Paris, 1947). He is unwilling to accord to Novalis' "speculation (on est tenté de dire: ses jongleries)" (p. 104) any validity except in contexts of mystical thought.

Edgar Hederer in his book on *Novalis* (Wien, 1949), esp. pp. 213-217, that emphasizes such facets as "Schicksal und Gemüt," "Magie," "Der Weg ins Innere," and "Christus und Sophie," concludes categorically and significantly: "Hardenbergs Fragmente über die Mathematik enthüllen die letzte Absicht seines Denkens und seiner Wissenschaft" (p. 214). But he treats only those passages on mathematics that fall within the domain of Novalis' meditations on magic idealism.

As research progresses, more and more significance is being attached to Novalis' fragments on mathematics. Friedrich Hiebel in his study *Novalis: der Dichter der blauen Blume* (Bern, 1951), is more concerned with Novalis' poems and novels than with his other fragments. Yet he is aware of our problem: "Bei Goethe waren Philosophie, Mathematik und Musik Welten, welche ihn nur von aussen und an der Peripherie seines Weltbildes zu bewegen vermochten, für Novalis aber waren sie Ausgangspunkte und Leitsterne seiner inneren Orientierung" (p. 73). However, the second part of his following claim is perhaps somewhat exaggerated: "Seine mathematischen Fragmente zeigen eine solche Originalität, dass sogar die heutige Novalisforschung ihn auch darin Pionierforschung leisten sieht" (p. 150). Like Gode- von Aesch, he admits in his following remark in a footnote that he cannot deal with mathematics in the framework of his study: "Die wesentlichen Fragmente des Novalis über Mathematik finden hier keinen besonderen Raum der Erwähnung und Darstellung" (p. 319).

Mention should be made of Ewald Wasmuth's article "Novalis' Beitrag zu einer 'Physik in einem höheren Sinne,'" *Neue Schweizer Rundschau*, Neue Folge, XVIII (1950-51), pp. 533-546. Wasmuth discusses the application of the concept of "Potenz" to a "higher physics."

Theodor Haering's monograph *Novalis als Philosoph* (Stuttgart, 1954) is the first comprehensive presentation of Novalis' philosophy. He deals with mathematics mainly in the twelve-page *Exkurs* "Novalis und die Mathematik" (pp. 541-552). He states somewhat apologetically that he will attempt to deal with this problem, but hastens to add that he does so with no claim to finality or conclusiveness. He rejects Käte Hamburger's identification of Novalis' conception of mathematics and physics with that of modern mathematics and physics. He draws a line between Novalis' higher "dialectic" mathematics and the conventional "rational" mathematics, a separation which, in this extreme form, is not justifiable. Haering makes Novalis appear too much as a critic of conventional mathematics. The difficult hymns to mathematics are not explained, but referred to Novalis' "higher, dialectic" mathematics (see the author's review article on Haering's book in *Comparative Literature*, VIII (1956), 264-268).

Thus Novalis' fragments on mathematics have been described by the various scholars at the various stages of research as utterances of a juggler of mystical concepts (Dilthey, Besset), as sporadic articulations of a morbid mind (Olshausen), as curious assertions of a person not in control of his reasoning powers (Haym), as peculiar (Gode- von Aesch), as going too far (L. E. Wagner), but also as pioneer work in modern mathematics (Hamburger, Hiebel), as revelatory of the ultimate goal of Novalis' thought (Hederer, Hiebel). Some authors prefer to ignore the problem (Heilborn, Havenstein), some state that for various reasons they are unable or unwilling to deal with it (Gode- von Aesch, Hiebel, Wagner), or are not yet ready to deal with it (Haering). This state of research with its conflicting opinions calls for an investigation of Novalis' relation to mathematics. It was demanded by Kluckhohn twenty-seven years ago (III, 10), and also by Samuel (*Der handschr. Nachlass...*, pp. 3, 44).

CHAPTER II

THE IMPACT OF MATHEMATICS ON NOVALIS

1. SOME ASPECTS OF THE HISTORY OF MATHEMATICS IN THE EIGHTEENTH CENTURY

> Unfortunately, the mechanical way in which calculus is sometimes taught fails to present the subject as the outcome of a dramatic intellectual struggle which has lasted for twenty-five hundred years or more, which is deeply rooted in many phases of human endeavor, and which will continue as long as man strives to understand himself as well as nature (foreword, Carl Boyer, *The Concepts of Calculus*, New York, 1949).
>
> R. COURANT, 1949

We noted in the preceding chapter that Novalis' observations on mathematics are philosophical, and, from the strictly mathematical point of view, unrigorous. We should also note, however, that a distinction must be made between the strictly mathematical point of view of the twentieth-century mathematician and the looser and more experimental attitude toward mathematics of his eighteenth-century predecessor. A mathematician may grant the appropriateness of this distinction and yet be inclined to ask why Novalis studied the works of such relatively unknown mathematicians as Burja, Büsch, Rehbein, Töpfer, Hindenburg, and Kästner, as a list of books in his possession indicates (see Section 4). Why did he not concentrate on such mathematical giants as Euler, Lagrange, Laplace, Jacob and Johann Bernoulli? The answer lies partly in the fact that many papers of the latter mathematicians were buried in such ponderous publications as the *Acta Eruditorum*, a journal published 1682-1782 in Leipzig, and the memoirs of the Academies of Science in Berlin and St. Petersburg. There is evidence that Novalis was acquainted with some of Euler's work (see Section 4), although in Novalis' published fragments there is only one specific reference to him in a general context (III, 67). Most great mathematicians in the eighteenth century were engaged in research at the Academies of Science and not teaching in universities. Two exceptions were the University at Göttingen and the École Polytechnique. At these institutions the study of mathematics became prominent toward the end of the eighteenth century. However,

Novalis studied at the Universities at Jena, Leipzig, Wittenberg, and at the Mining Academy at Freiberg. In contradistinction to the greater mathematicians, such lesser mathematicians as Burja, Büsch, and Rehbein published watered-down and popularized versions of the results obtained by the former group of mathematicians. A similar procedure is followed today. In France, more texts were published by the greater mathematicians. We find in Novalis' possession copies of Lagrange's *Théorie des fonctions analytique* (1797) and Laplace's popular, non-mathematical *Exposition du système du monde* (1796), both in German translation: *Theorie der analytischen Funktionen, in welcher die Grundsätze der Differentialrechnung vorgetragen werden*. Aus dem Französischen von Gruson (Berlin, 1798), 2 Bände; and *Darstellung des Weltsystems*. Aus dem Französischen von J. K. F. Hauff (Frankfurt, 1797-98), 2 Bände. The inaccessibility of the results of current research in mathematics at the time of Novalis is also accentuated by the fact that the first German mathematical journal in continuous existence, the *Journal für reine und angewandte Mathematik* (Berlin & Leipzig), was founded by A. L. Crelle in 1826, *i.e.*, twenty-five years after Novalis' death (see Wilhelm Lorey, "August Crelle zum Gedächtnis," *Journal für die reine und angewandte Mathematik*, Vol. 157 (1926), p. 3). The only regularly published mathematical journal that Novalis could have consulted is the *Journal de l'École polytechnique*, founded in 1794. Novalis' mathematics teacher in Leipzig, K. F. Hindenburg, founded with Johann Bernoulli in 1786 the *Leipziger Magazin für reine und angewandte Mathematik*, but the undertaking failed after three years of publication. Only a popular mathematical journal like *The Ladies Diary or the Woman's Almanac, containing many delightful and entertaining particulars, peculiarly adapted for the use and diversion of the fair sex*, published since 1704, managed to survive for over a century.

With regard to the lack of rigor and the mingling of philosophy with mathematics in the thought of Novalis, it should be pointed out that in the eighteenth century "there was general doubt as to the nature of the foundations of the methods of fluxions and the differential calculus" (Boyer, p. 224). "The whole question of the foundation of calculus remained a subject of debate and so did all questions relating to infinite processes. The 'mystical' period in the foundation of mathematics itself provoked a mysticism which occasionally went far beyond that of the founding fathers" (Dirk J. Struik, *A Concise History of Mathematics*, New York, 1948, II, 176). Novalis also grappled with the concept of infinity (see Chapters III & IV) and spoke of mystical (II, 333) and magical (III, 295) mathematics.

The philosophical setting of the mathematical achievements in the seventeenth and eighteenth centuries may be best illustrated by the figure of Leibniz, one of the founders of calculus. He searched for a "scientia generalis" and made discoveries in mathematics. He searched for a "characteristica generalis" and was led to permutations, combinations, and to plans for a theory of mathematical logic. "His invention of the calculus must be understood against his philosophical background; it was the result of his search for a "lingua generalis" of change and of motion in particular" (Struik, II, 156). He was stimulated by the study of Descartes and Pascal. Descartes' results in the analytic geometry were only an illustration of his new method, of his search for a "mathesis universalis" that would encompass all knowledge. Novalis' "Arithmetica universalis" (III, 23-25) is intended as a direct continuation of Descartes' "mathesis universalis" and Leibniz' "scientia generalis." Novalis pursued the original goals of these philosopher-mathematicians. Guided by their grand aims, he set out to mathematize all branches of knowledge. His efforts were directed toward a rough outline of a universal encyclopedia in which all knowledge was to be integrated into a unified mathematical pattern. He had no intention to confine himself to the more limited sphere of mathematics proper, and therefore it is unfair to evaluate his thought on mathematics in strict mathematical terms. Novalis' pronouncements on calculus are vague from the modern point of view, but so were many of Leibniz' and Newton's (Struik, II, 158). A new basis of differential calculus was offered by Euler in his *Institutiones calculi differentialis* (1755), the most widely used text in calculus before the publication of Lagrange's *Théorie des fonctions analytiques* (1797). However, Struik reminds us: "It is instructive to point out not only some of Euler's contributions to science but also some of his weaknesses. Infinite processes were still carelessly handled in the eighteenth century and much of the work of the leading mathematicians of that period impresses us as wildly enthusiastic experimentation. There was experimentation with infinite series, with the use of symbols such as $0, \infty, \sqrt{-1},\ldots$" (II, 175). In a similar fashion, Novalis experimented with the symbols of 0 and ∞ (see, for example, III, 36, 102, 247). Struik further points out that we cannot follow Euler when he writes

$$1 - 3 + 5 - 7 + \ldots = 0,$$ or when he concludes from

$$n + n^2 + \ldots = \frac{n}{1-n}$$

and $$1 + \frac{1}{n} + \frac{1}{n^2} + \ldots = \frac{n}{n-1}$$

that $\quad \ldots + \dfrac{1}{n^2} + \dfrac{1}{n} + 1 + n + n^2 + \ldots = 0.$

Moreover, Struik calls attention to the defects of Euler's way of basing the calculus on the introduction of zeros of different orders. "An infinitesimally small quantity, wrote Euler in his *Institutiones calculi differentialis*, in 1755, is truly zero" (Struik, II, 176).

Novalis associates mathematics in various manners with religion. This seems strange and irrelevant today, but was common in the seventeenth and eighteenth centuries. Most of the great mathematicians of that time were religious, for example, Newton, the Bernoullis, and Euler. They did not hesitate to relate mathematical concepts to religious problems. To cite an extreme yet characteristic example, Jacob Bernoulli noticed that a certain spiral always regained its original shape by various geometric transformations. Thus the spiral became to him a symbol of resurrection and he had it put on his tombstone (see Otto Spiess, *Leonhard Euler, ein Beitrag zur Geistesgeschichte des achtzehnten Jahrhunderts*, Frauenfeld & Leipzig, 1929, p. 20). Leibniz remarked that all numbers could be represented by the two digits 0 and 1 in the binary system of notation and thought of the creation of the world by God (1) from Nothing (0) (*Ibid.*) A similar "mathematical" description or "explanation" of God's creation was offered by Guido Grandi, a monk and professor at Pisa, known for his study of rosaces ($r = sinn\theta$) and other curves resembling flowers. He considered the formula

$$\tfrac{1}{2} = 1 - 1 + 1 - 1 + 1 - \ldots$$
$$= (1-1) + (1-1) + (1-1) + \ldots$$
$$= 0 \;\; + \;\; 0 \;\; + \;\; 0 \;\; + \ldots$$

as the symbol of creation from Nothing. He obtained the result $\tfrac{1}{2}$ by considering two sons who inherit a gem from their father. Each may keep it for one year in alternation, hence each possesses half of it, or each possesses it half the time (Struik, II, 177). Novalis, likewise, speaks of "Schöpfung ex nihilo et ex aliquo" (III, 226).

Newton devoted himself to theology and considered such pursuit to be more important than his scientific achievements. Toward the end of his life he attempted to prove that the prophecies of Daniel and the poetry of the Apocalypse made sense. He also tried to harmonize the dates of the Old Testament with those of history (see Morris Kline, *Mathematics in Western Culture*, New York, 1953, p. 260). He argued for the existence of God along the lines that the well-ordered universe implies a creator (Kline, p. 260).

J. F. Montucla in his *Histoire des mathematiques*, 2nd ed. (Paris, 1799), I, 35-36, discusses the application and misapplication of mathematics to theology in his age. After ridiculing a certain Caramuel de Lobkowitz who wrote a *Mathesis audax* in which he attempted to elucidate through mathematics the most abstruse problems of metaphysics and religion, Montucla states in a footnote, in an obvious attempt to avoid incurring the displeasure of the theologians: "Nous remarquons, cependant, que quelques auteurs ont travaillé d'une manière plus judicieuse à faire voir l'usage de mathématiques dans l'étude de la théologie et de l'écriture sainte." Then he proceeds to list various mathematical works relating to theology, such as Georg Arnold's *Sacra mathesis* (Altorf, 1676), L. C. Sturm's *Mathesis ad sacrae scripturae interpretationem applicata* (1710), J. J. Schmid's *Biblischer mathematicus seu illustration sacrae scripturae ex mathematicis scientiis* (1736), and others.

Montucla also deals with books purporting to mathematize medicine. He writes: "Le fameux médecin écossois [Archibald] Pitcairn a aussi entrepris, dans un de ses ouvrages, d'élever la médecine à la certitude mathématique *(Elementa medicinae physico-mathematica.* London 1717)" (I, 37). A similar attempt was made by Novalis in a fragment under the heading "Mathematische Physiologie" (III, 129-132) and in other fragments dealing with "medizinische Algeber oder Analysis" (III, 233) and "Regeln der physiologischen Algeber" (III, 90).

In the eighteenth century mathematics was also applied to ethics. Maupertuis, a mathematician of high rank, who was appointed by Frederick the Great to direct the Academy of Science in Berlin, designated the good as a positive quantity, and evil as negative. The distribution of good and evil in human society is to him a huge algebraic equation, and it is the task of the governments to make the positive prevail (see H. E. Timerding, *Die Verbreitung mathematischen Wissens und mathematischer Auffassung,* Berlin & Leipzig, 1914, p. 104). In a similar manner, Compte de Buffon offered a "moral arithmetic" in his *Essai d'arithmetique morale* (1777) as a supplement to his work on natural history (see F. Cajori, *A History of Mathematics,* 2nd ed., New York, 1929, p. 243). Condorcet made a mathematical inquiry into the credibility of extraordinary historical facts. Condillac wrote in 1798 that all mental activities of man are an operation for certain sensations, and in his philosophy he attempted to extend mathematical symbols to all thinking (Timerding, pl. 104). La Mettrie claimed to have discovered the calculus of the human mind, and the French economist Francois Quesnay announced equations for economic and social life (Kline, p. 238). These endeavors reveal the forces of Rationalism and Enlightenment in the eighteenth century. "It seemed only a matter of time before all phenomena, natural, social and mental, would be reduced to mathematical laws" (*Ibid*). "The chief characteristic of this new approach to knowledge was unbounded confidence in reason and the validity of the extension of mathematical methods throughout the physical and formal sciences and beyond them to all fields of knowledge" (Kline, p. 239). It is against this background that Novalis' seemingly fantastic plan to mathematize all branches of knowledge and to unify them in a universal encyclopedia must be considered. Abraham Gotthelf Kästner, Georg Christoph Lichtenberg, Goethe, Herder, and a number of Romanticists are among prominent eighteenth-century figures concerned with the union of the most disparate branches of knowledge, for example, the physical sciences and the humanities (see, for example, the present author's studies "Goethe's Views on Pure Mathematics," *Germanic Review*, XXXI, 49-69 and "Goethe's Thought in the Light of His Pronouncements on Applied and Misapplied Mathematics," *PMLA*, LXXIII, 505-515). For general discussion of science in German Romanticism the reader is referred to W. Bietak, editor, *Romantische Wissenschaft* (Leipzig, 1940) and A. Gode- von Aesch, *Natural Science in German Romanticism* (New York, 1941).

2. NOVALIS' STUDY OF MATHEMATICS AND HIS ACQUAINTANCE WITH MATHEMATICIANS

After this brief portrayal of the position of mathematics in some general cultural contexts of eighteenth-century Europe, and before discussing Novalis' fragments on mathematics in detail, we shall consider how much mathematics Novalis actually knew, and when, where, and under whom he studied this subject.

Novalis was born on May 2, 1772, at Oberwiederstedt (or Wiederstedt), southeast of the Harz mountains in central Germany. He was a fragile and passive child until the age of nine, when a serious illness transformed him into an alert and gifted boy who was eager to learn as much as he could (see Paul Kluckhohn, "Friedrich von Hardenbergs Entwicklung und Dichtung," I, 11*. Most biographical data will be taken from this standard study). He entered the "Prima," *i.e.*, the uppermost form, of the Luthergymnasium at Eisleben on June 17, 1790, but left the institution on October 5 of the same year, after the death of the rector of the school, David Christian Jani, the famous Horace scholar who had been the main attraction of the school. One can hardly speak of mathematical instruction at such Gymnasien in the eighteenth century (Timerding, p. 108). In 1735 no examination in mathematics was required at the "Abiturientenexamen," the final comprehensive high school examination, in Prussia, and only on July 12, 1810, *i.e.*, nine years after Novalis' death, was legislature introduced in Prussia to give the mathematics teacher full and equal status in the high schools. Similar conditions prevailed in other parts of Germany. Previously, attempts to teach mathematics, as distinct from the rudiments of arithmetic, in high school had been sporadic. In 1812 the Prussian School Decrees required that an examination be given in the following mathematical subjects at the "Abiturientenexamen:" elementary arithmetic and algebra, equations of the first and second degree, logarithms, elementary geometry as contained in books 1-6, 11, 12 of Euclid's *Elements*, plane trigonometry, and the use of mathematical tables (Timerding, p. 114). However, for a lack of teachers and the lofty contempt for mathematics on the part of some teachers of classics who still held sway over the high schools, these official requirements were not met. Since Novalis' few months of high school attendance fall into the year 1790, it is very unlikely that any knowledge of mathematics beyond the level of elementary arithmetic and geometry had been expected of him at this time.

On October 3, 1790, Novalis was matriculated at the University at Jena, where he stayed to the end of September 1791. He was officially registered in the faculty of law, but devoted himself mainly to the study of literature and philosophy. Notable teachers were Reinhold, the expositor of Kantian philosophy, and Schiller, then professor of history at Jena. On October 5, 1791, he wrote to Reinhold from Goseck: "Ich werde in drei Wochen nach Leipzig abgehen und nach einer gänzlich veränderten Lebensordnung zu leben dort anfangen. Jurisprudenz, Mathematik, und Philosophie sollen die drei Wissenschaften sein, denen ich diesen Winter mich mit Leib und Seele ergeben will und im strengsten Sinne ergebe. Ich muss mehr Festigkeit, mehr Bestimmtheit, mehr Plan, mehr Zweck mir zu erringen suchen, und dies kann ich am leichtesten durch ein strenges Studium dieser Wissenschaften erlangen. Seelenfasten in Absicht der schönen Wissenschaften und gewissenhafte Enthaltsamkeit von allem Zweckwidrigen habe ich mir zum strengsten Gesetz gemacht" (IV, 26). He arrived in Leipzig the same month and enrolled in the famous university of that city. As in Jena, his formal intent was the study of law, but he also attended lectures on mathematics and the natural sciences.

The study of mathematics at German universities was very sporadic and unorganized in the eighteenth century. It improved during the middle of the century at Helmstedt and Göttingen. At the University at Jena, for example, the level remained low for a long time. The following announcement of courses for the winter semester 1802/3 illuminates this point: Introduction to the Study of Mathematics; Theoretical and Practical Arithmetic; Popular Astronomy, and so on. The level of instruction in these courses was lower than in the upper forms of a modern German high school.

When Goethe, like Novalis, came to Leipzig as a law student in 1765, *i.e.*, twenty-six years earlier, he attended the lectures in "mathesis pura," required at that time of all students entering the higher faculties (see Wilhelm Lorey, "Goethes Stellung zur Mathematik," *Goethe als Seher und Erforscher der Natur*, ed. Johannes Walther, Weimar, 1930, p. 133). Novalis possibly had to comply with the same requirement. Whatever the case may be, his letter quoted above indicates his intention to study mathematics at Leipzig. The study of mathematics as a major subject, the "Fachstudium," began in Germany around 1800, although a course on the integral calculus had been announced at the University of Leipzig by Professor Bortz as early as 1777 (see Wilhelm Lorey, *Das Studium der Mathematik an den deutschen Universitäten seit dem Anfang des neunzehnten Jahrhunderts*, Leipzig & Berlin, 1916, p. 24). On the other hand, K. B. Mollweide whose teaching career in mathematics at the University at Leipzig began in 1804, and whom Gauss regarded as a thorough mathematician, was convinced that higher mathematics could not be taught in a class room because it involved too much writing on the blackboard.

At the time of Novalis' stay in Leipzig, Karl Friedrich Hindenburg (1741-1808) taught mathematics at the university. There can hardly be any doubt that Novalis attended his lectures. Olshausen states that Novalis' serious study of mathematics probably began later at Freiberg, but that "schon in Leipzig hätte er Gelegenheit gehabt, den Mann zu hören, dessen Ideen, und noch mehr die seiner Schule, ihn jetzt stark zu bewegen begannen: Hindenburg, den systematischen Ausgestalter der kombinatorischen Analysis und den Begründer der kombinatorischen Schule" (Olshausen, p. 52). Hindenburg had attended the Gymnasium at Freiberg and come to the University at Leipzig in 1757, where he, not unlike Novalis, "in buntem Gemisch Arzneikunst und Philosophie, alte Literatur und Physik, Mathematik und Aesthetik studierte" (see Cantor's article in *Allgemeine deutsche Biographie*, XII). Hindenburg had studied under the poet Gellert in Leipzig and the poet-mathematician Kästner in Göttingen. Hence Novalis must have found a congenial mind in him. Hindenburg obtained his master's degree in Leipzig in 1771 and became in 1781 extraordinary professor of philosophy at the same university – another reason why his broad education must have appealed to Novalis. Hindenburg had first devoted himself to philological studies and had published two treatises on this subject in 1763 and 1769. In 1785 he applied for a professorship of Greek and Latin which had become vacant in Leipzig, again displaying a versatility and universality of interest similar to Novalis' wide range of endeavor. He did not get the position, but filled a vacancy in physics in 1786. He held this post until his death in 1808, but taught and published mainly in the field of mathematics. Novalis came to Leipzig in 1791 and very probably was in personal contact with Hindenburg. Novalis had among his books Hindenburg's *Novi Systematis permutationum, combinationum etc. primae lineae* (Leipzig, 1781) and *Der polynomische Lehrsatz* (Leipzig, 1796) as well as Kästner's *Anfangsgründe der Analysis des Unendlichen* (Göttingen, 1760, 3. Aufl. 1799) (see IV, 476 ff.). In the history of mathematics Hindenburg is known as the founder of the combinatorial school which concentrated on combinatorial analysis, a subject first treated coherently by Leibniz in his dissertation *Ars Combinatoria* in 1668. Olshausen traces this branch of mathematics further to the "ars magna" of Ramon Lull (c. 1236-1315), the Catalan philosopher who set forth a method of expressing all knowledge by the manipulation of symbols. Such a manipulation of symbols resulted in various combinations and permutations of ideas and was expected to lead to new discoveries. It is to this origin, as well as to Leibniz' search for an "ars inveniendi" that Olshausen traces Novalis' identification of mathematical analysis with "Erfindungskunst" (Olshausen, p. 53). The fragment in question is the following: "Die Analysis ist (die Divinations- oder) die Erfindungskunst auf Regeln gebracht. – Ihre mögliche Ausbreitung und Vervollkommnung" (III, 162, *Das allgemeine Brouillon*, Nr. 567 [1798/99]). Another fragment reads: "So wie sich andere Grössen finden lassen – so müssen sich auch Formeln berechnen lassen – Formelnerfindungskunst. (Instrumentenerfindungskunst). Vielleicht will dies die kombinatorische Analysis tun. Dann wäre sie sehr hoch. – Die kombinatorische Analysis der Physik wäre die indirekte Erfindungskunst, die Baco gesucht hat" (III, 23).

In Cantor's history of mathematics the aims of the so-called combinatorial school are described as follows: "Nach diesen Ergebnissen [*i.e.*, after the results of the Bernoullis, Moivre, Euler] kommen wir zu einer merkwürdigen Epoche, zu der sogenannten *kombinatorischen Schule*. Die ausgesprochene Absicht der sie begründenden und fördernden Männer war, neben die gewöhnlichen Operationen der Arithmetik, Algebra und Analysis die kombinatorischen Operationen als gleichberechtigt und gleichwertig zu stellen und für sie das Bürgerrecht zu erwerben... Diese Schule fasste trotz ihrer grossen Ziele und Absichten nur in Deutschland Boden und trug auch hier nur bescheidene Früchte; von grossen Forschern im mathematischen Bereiche gehörte ihr keiner an... das meiste von dem, was sie brachte, sank sobald in eine nicht immer ganz gerechte Vergessenheit" (Cantor, IV, 201).

One of Hindenburg's first mathematical treatises is the *Beschreibung einer ganz neuen Art, nach einem bekannten Gesetze fortgehende Zahlen durch Abzählen oder Abmessen bequem und sicher zu finden*, published in 1776. In this treatise he attempts to employ the so-called sieve of Eratosthenes which enables one to read off the terms of an arithmetical series. Similar ideas are found in Novalis' fragments: "Wenige bekannte Glieder, durch die man instand gesetzt wird, eine unendliche Menge unbekannter Glieder zu finden, – machen die Konstruktionsformel aus" (III, 38, *Freiberger Studien* [1798/99]).

Some of Hindenburg's early works on combinatorial analysis, in particular the above-mentioned *Der polynomische Lehrsatz*, deal with the multinomial theorem, or, as it was called at that time, "die Potenzierung des Infinitinoms." Novalis lists under "Materialien" for his "Arithmetica universalis": "Klügel, aus dem 'Polynomischen Lehrsatz' von Hindenburg... Hindenburgs Schriften und andere mehr" (III, 23). The high hopes that Hindenburg cherished about his combinatorial analysis were transferred by Novalis to his universal arithmetic. "Welche unerschöpfliche Menge zu neuen individuellen Kombinationen liegt nicht umher! Wer einmal dieses Geheimnis erraten hat, der hat nichts mehr nötig als den Entschluss, der unendlichen Mannigfaltigkeit und ihrem blossen Genusse zu entsagen und irgendwo anzufangen" (II, 326). He explicitly states in *Das allgemeine Brouillon*, Nr. 246 (III, 99): "Die kombinatorische Analytik gehört eigentlich zur universellen Arithmetik." Klügel, whom Novalis also mentions in his "Materialien" for the universal arithmetic, states in a contribution to Hindenburg's *Der polynomische Lehrsatz*: "Die Analysis endlicher Grössen besteht aus zwei Hauptteilen, die zwar durch gegenseitige Hilfleistungen mit einander verbunden sind, aber nicht einer auf dem anderen beruhen... Diese beiden Teile sind die Algebra und die Analysis im engern Verstande" (p. 48). Similarly, Novalis states in connection with the combinatorial analysis and with this passage of Klügel: "Sie, die Algebra und die sog(enannte) Analysis machen eine Wissenschaft aus" (III, 99).

Hindenburg was the first to set up, in his works on combinatorial analysis, simple rules for the formation of tables of permutations, combinations, and variations, in order to prevent omissions or duplications in writing them. These rules were also meant to afford an easy transition from the combinations or permutations of n elements to a set of $n + 1$ elements. Here is one of Hindenburg's examples:

```
           c      b      a
           4      3      2      1
                                ──a
           4      3      1      2
                                  b
           4      2      3      1
           4      2      1      3
           4      1      3      2
           4      1      2      3
                                  c
           3      4      2      1
           3      4      1      2
           3      2      4      1
           3      2      1      4
           3      1      4      2
           3      1      2      4     (Cantor, IV, 209)
```

Novalis applies a similar rule in writing down all possible variants of a dialectic pattern of reasoning in order to make the reasoning complete and exhaustive (Theodor Haering would probably regard this as an instance of Novalis' "higher, dialectic mathematics" – see Chapter I, Section 3). Novalis represents the terms thesis, antithesis, and synthesis as follows:

$$a = a \quad - \quad These$$
$$b = a \quad - \quad Antithese$$
$$c = a + b \; -Synthese \qquad \text{(II, 156)}$$

Then he proceeds:
"Die Synthesis kann nun

1. von a (dem einen Gegensatze) zu b (dem anderen Gegensatze), von b zu c als dem Gemeinsatze und von c zu a gehen.
2. von a zu c — von c zu b — von b zu a.
3. von a zu b — dann von a zu c — dann von c zu b.
4. von $a - b + a - c + b - c$
5. $a - c + a - b + b - c$
6. $a - c + a - b + c - b$
7. $c - a + a - b + b - c$
8. $c - b + b - a + a - c$
9. $c - a + c - b + a - b$
10. $c - a + c - b + b - a$
11. $c - b + c - a + a - b$
12. $c - b + c - a + b - a$ " (II, 157)

Other examples are found in II, 253ff. In the above example the signs — and + do not denote the conventional "minus" or "plus," respectively, but serve as abbreviations of the copulae as defined in

30

1, 2, and 3. (cf. in this connection Chapter IV, Section "Mathematics and Philosophy").

In 1791 there appeared in Halle a study entitled *Theorie der Dimensionszeichen nebst ihrer Anwendung auf verschiedene Materialien aus der Analysis endlicher Grössen* by Ernst Gottfried Fischer of the Academy of Science in Berlin. This study caused quite an uproar, because it reported the invention of combinatorial analysis, whereas actually it contained nothing more than Hindenburg's version of the subject disguised in different notation. Heinrich August Töpfer, a student of Hindenburg's, set out to expose the supposed plagiator by exhibiting the priority of Hindenburg in the presentation of the subject matter, in his highly polemical book *Combinatorische Analytik und Theorie der Dimensionszeichen in Parallele gestellt* (Leipzig, 1793). Fischer protested in 1794 that he had obtained his results independently. He was supported in his claim by Abel Burja, Professor of Mathematics at the Academie militaire in Berlin and a member of the Academy of Science. Novalis owned copies of both these works. Various other references indicate that he was familiar with the controversy. A year after Novalis' death, Fischer's independence from Hindenburg was conclusively demonstrated by Johann Friedrich Pfaff (under whom Gauss had completed his doctorate at the University at Helmstedt in 1799), then Professor of Mathematics at the University of Halle.

Thus we have shown, among other things, that (1) circumstances in Leipzig indicate that Novalis must have studied mathematics under Hindenburg; (2) there are many points of contact between Hindenburg's combinatorial analysis and Novalis' fragments on universal arithmetic; (3) Novalis puts Hindenburg's name at the head of the list of materials for his contemplated universal arithmetic; (4) he was in possession of Hindenburg's major mathematical works and other studies relating to the combinatorial school; (5) Novalis went to Leipzig with the stated intention of studying mathematics, in addition to law and philosophy; (6) Hindenburg taught the mathematics courses at Leipzig at the time of Novalis' study at this university. Hence we disagree with Olshausen's assumption that Novalis' serious study of mathematics began not at Leipzig, but four years later at Freiberg. There can hardly be any doubt that, before coming to Freiberg, he had already received a considerable grounding in this subject during his stay in Leipzig.

On March 10, 1793, Novalis left Leipzig for Wittenberg, where he passed his law examinations at the university on June 14, 1794. From October 25, 1794 to February 6, 1796 he was engaged as a law clerk to the District Justiciary A. C. Just at Tennstedt.

Soon after the appearance of Fichte's *Grundlage der gesamten Wissenschaftslehre* in its first published version (1794), Novalis immersed intensively in the thought of this philosopher. Through Reinhold in Jena and Friedrich Schlegel in Leipzig he had become acquainted with Kant. Novalis' "Philosophische Studien 1795/97" (II, 103-308) reflect his intensive "Auseinandersetzung" with these two philosophers. A number of his fragments on mathematics resulted from his grappling with their ideas (see Section 3 for details).

In 1794 the twenty-two-year old Novalis was introduced to the twelve-year old Sophie von Kühn at nearby Grüningen. They fell in love and became engaged on March 15, 1795. In the fall of the same year Sophie became ill; she died of consumption on March 19, 1797. During Sophie's long illness, Novalis turned to Spinoza, a philosopher, who, like Novalis, had attempted to mathematize ethics in his *Ethica ordine geometrica demonstrata* (Amsterdam, 1677) by employing a systematic set of definitions, axioms, and theorems. During the few most trying weeks before Sophie's death, Novalis sought consolation in mathematics. This is clearly indicated by his notes in a copy of a calendar for the year 1797, as reprinted in IV, 377-8:

Jan. 11, 1797 "Math(ematik). Phil(osophie) / Erzählung..."
Jan. 12 "Math(ematik). Phil(osophie)..."
Jan. 13 "Math(ematik). Phil(osophie)..."
Jan. 14 "Math(ematik). Phil(osophie). / 'Pensées (of Pascal).."
March 10 "Heute früh sah ich sie zum letzten Male."
March 19 "Heute früh halb 10 ist sie gestorben. –
15 Jahr und 2 Tage alt. – geb. 1782"

The function of mathematics and other sciences as sources of solace and alleviation in his sorrow before and after Sophie's death becomes even more apparent from Novalis' consolatory letter to his brother Erasmus at the time of the latter's illness: "Dein Entschluss, Algebra zu studieren, ist gewiss sehr heilsam. Die Wissenschaften haben wunderbare Heilkräfte – wenigstens stillen sie, wie Opiate, die Schmerzen und erheben uns in Sphären, die ein ewiger Sonnenschein umgibt. Sie sind die schönste Freistätte, die uns gegönnt ward. Ohne diesen Trost wollt ich und könnt ich nicht leben. Wie hätt ich ohne sie seit anderthalb Jahren so gelassen S(ophiens) Krankheit zusehn und ausserdem so manchen Verdriesslichkeiten ausgesetzt sein können? Es mag mir begegnen was will; die Wissenschaften bleiben mir – mit ihnen hoff ich alles Ungemach des Lebens zu bestehn." This letter was written less than two months before Sophie's death, on February 26, 1797 (IV, 177). On May 26, 1797, he noted in his diary: "Früh Fichtes 'Naturlehre.' – Spazieren – viel Gutes gedacht – Zu Hause traf ich Karolinchen krank. Sie besserte sich bald – Ich schwatzte abends viel von Chemie und Mathematik durcheinander" (IV, 390). Mathematics gave Novalis a firm prop to cling to, for he wrote: "Gegen Ängstlichkeit, i.e., gegen willkürliche Wahnbegriffe muss ich auf der Hut sein" (June 11, 1797, IV, 394). Novalis now wanted to join Sophie in the Hereafter. His love for Sophie merged with religion and philosophy. He took the word "philosophy" in its literal meaning: "love of Sophie." He mingled religion with mathematics. The entry of January 14, 1797 suggests that he turned once more to a philosopher-mathematician for consolation: Pascal's *Pensée sur la religion*. Pascal had juxtaposed mathematics and religion, Novalis attempted to fuse them (see Chapter IV, Section "Mathematics and Religion"). After Sophie's death Novalis devoted himself with even greater fervor to the abstract sciences. August Wilhelm Schlegel wrote to Goethe about Novalis on September 24, 1797, from Jena: "Seine Schwermut hat ihn mit doppelter Tätigkeit in die abstraktesten Wissenschaften gestürzt" (I, 25*). Novalis again devoted himself to philosophy, especially Kant and Fichte, and to mathematics. At this time he also delved into the works of the Dutch philosopher Franz Hemsterhuis (1722-1790), with whose thought he had already become acquainted in Leipzig. Although, on the whole, Hemsterhuis is an advocate of irrationalism, Novalis excerpted from his *Lettre sur l'homme et ses rapports* (*Oeuvres philosophiques*, Paris, 1809, I, 135 ff.) the following statements, translating them from the original French: "Die Volkommenheit unserer Wissenschaft wird nach ihrer Kapazität für Mathematik beurteilt" and "Objekt und Idee der Anschauung ist in der Mathematik eins" (II, 289) Novalis comments on them as follows: "Die Wissenschaften sind nur aus Mangel an Genie und Scharfsinn getrennt – die Verhältnisse zwischen ihnen sind dem Verstand und Stumpfsinn zu verwickelt und entfernt voneinander. Die grössten Wahrheiten unserer Tage verdanken wir solchen Kombinationen der lange getrennten Glieder der Totalwissenschaft" (II, 289). Novalis, although deeply concerned with the systematic presentation of the various branches of knowledge, never lost historical perspective, retrospectively or prospectively. He was convinced that at one time all sciences were united, but that it had become necessary to unite again the long separated members of the total science, which had drifted apart, because their relations had become too involved for our minds. From Hemsterhuis' *Aristée* (*Oeuvres philos.*, II, 9 ff.) Novalis translated the following observation on axioms: "Axiomen beruhn auf sinnlicher Überzeugung. Die künstliche, gemachte Überzeugung geht vom Axiom aus. Die letztere hat die erstere verdrängt" (II, 293). Hemsterhuis' observation is in agreement with Novalis' pronouncement: "Die Mathematik ist echte Wissenschaft, weil sie gemachte Kenntnisse enthält" (III, 270). Thus Novalis' thought was stimulated by some of Hemsterhuis' ideas. During this time Novalis also studied Plotinus, Jakob Böhme, and Eckartshausen. His "mystische Fragmente" originated on the basis of this study and of his experience of Sophie's death (I, 27*).

From December 1, 1797 to Whitsuntide 1799 Novalis was a student at the famous Mining Academy (Bergakademie) at Freiberg in preparation for his intended career in salt works administration. The "königlich Sächsische Bergakademie zu Freiberg" had been founded in 1766 by Friedrich Anton von Heynitz, an uncle of Novalis. It was one of the first institutions in which the exact sciences were consistently applied to technology (see *Die königlich Sächsische Bergakademie zu Freiberg*, Freiberg, 1904, p. 7). Novalis' most prominent teacher at Freiberg was Abraham Gottlob Werner (1750-1817), professor of mineralogy and mining engineering at the academy. One of the founders of the science of geology, he is known as the originator of the now obsolete Wernerian or "Neptunian" theory of the aqueous origin of the surface of the earth. He was the first to separate geology and mineralogy and to place geology on the basis of observation and experience. Some scholars trace Novalis' efforts toward systematization of all knowledge for his universal encyclopedia to Werner's systematization of geology in his own encyclopedia. This dependence is partial and indirect, despite Novalis' laudatory comments on Werner's encyclopedia (III, 188, 201, 208, 302, and II, 428) (see Haering, p. 125).

In addition to geology, mineralogy, and mining engineering, Novalis devoted himself to physics, mathematics, and chemistry at Freiberg. The last decade of the eighteenth century was a time of great discoveries and bold hypotheses in the natural sciences (I, 37*). Upon Priestley's discovery of oxygen the old phlogiston theory was discarded. Lavoisier elevated chemistry to the status of an exact science. Galvani's experiments with frogs led in 1789 to the discovery of "animal electricity." (see Wagner, p. 31). Novalis took a vital interest in these developments. He was fascinated by discoveries that turned alchemy into chemistry. If mere philosophical speculation on the nature of the universe had developed into physics, alchemy into chemistry, quackery into medicine, astrology into astronomy, and, more generally, speculative branches of knowledge into systematic sciences with empirical bases or logical structures, why should it not be possible to continue this process of emancipation and mathematize religion, magic, music, or even poetry? Such thoughts crossed Novalis' mind. There was excitement and expectation in the intellectual atmosphere of the time. No avenues were to be left unexplored. Novalis wrote to Friedrich Schlegel on November 7, 1798 from Freiberg: "Ich denke hier Wahrheiten und *Ideen im grossen – genialische* Gedanken – ein lebendiges, wissenschaftliches Organon hervorzubringen – und durch diese synkretische Politik der Intelligenz mir den Weg zur *echten Praxis* – dem wahrhaften Reunionsprozess – zu bahnen" (IV, 204 f.). Novalis noted the following in Freiberg during 1798/99:

> Gravitationslehre und Arithmetica universalis will ich zuerst durchgehen. Jener soll eine Stunde, dieser zwei Stunden gewidmet werden. Was mir nebenher einfällt, wird in das allgemeine Brouillon mit hineingeschrieben.
>
> Eine Stunde der Enzyklopädistik überhaupt. Diese enthält wissenschaftliche Algeber – Gleichungen – Verhältnisse – Ähnlichkeiten – Gleichheiten – Wirkungen der Wissenschaften aufeinander.
>
> Die Revision des Wernerschen Systems und die Kritik meines Unternehmens muss nun die erste Arbeit sein.
>
> (Bearbeitung der Logik – der Algeber etc. – gehört dann zur Tagesordnung). (IV, 399 f.)

Novalis must have written enthusiastically about these plans to A. W. Schlegel, and the latter, in his turn, must have expressed concern over Novalis' apparent abandonment of literary pursuits and his intense immersion into mathematics and the natural sciences, for Novalis wrote to him on February 24, 1798 from Freiberg: "Dann will ich Sie von der Besorgnis befreien, dass ich hier zu lauter a + b werde. Ich bin vielmehr wahrhaft entschlossen, die Mathematik künftig sehr verächtlich zu behandeln, weil sie mich wie einen Abcschützen behandelt" (IV, 228). This may be the expression of a momentary spell of disappointment arising from a discrepancy between his ambitious plans and hard reality, but it is certainly not to be interpreted as Novalis' intention to embrace henceforth poetry exclusively and give up philosophy and science. This common reading is also rejected by Haering in his recent comprehensive monograph on Novalis' philosophy (p. 552). During the summer of the year 1800, *i.e.*, less than a year before his death, Novalis made a note of a study plan for himself, with emphasis on the subjects rendered in spaced type in the Kluckhohn-Samuel edition of Novalis' works: "Studium der sächsischen Geschichte etc. Sachsens überhaupt. M a t h e m a t i k. A s t r o n o m i e. P h y s i k ..." (III, 336). Also, half a year before his death, on October 16, 1800, Novalis made this entry in his notebook: "Sonst reis ich viel mit dem Vater und bin fleissig in der Math(ematik) etc." (IV, 410).

At this time Novalis became acquainted with the works of Franz von Baader (1765-1841), the mystic Catholic theosophist, who, like Hemsterhuis, was an irrationalist, but stimulated some of Novalis' thought on mathematics (see next section). What appealed to Novalis in Baader was his search for a binding and unifying principle in the universe (I, 39*). Another congenial philosopher was

Schelling, whose ideas on the interrelation of nature and the spirit have points of contact with Novalis' "Realidealismus."

In December 1798 Novalis became engaged to Julie, the daughter of Johann Friedrich W. von Charpentier (1728-1805), professor of mathematics and drawing at the Mining Academy at Freiberg and Novalis' teacher in these subjects. Charpentier, like Novalis and Hindenburg, was more than a mathematician. Like Novalis, he had studied law at the University at Leipzig. At the same time he had delved into mathematics and attained such proficiency in this subject that he was appointed professor of mathematics at Freiberg in 1767. He is not mentioned by such authors of standard histories of mathematics as Cantor, Cajori, or Struik, yet in the *Allgemeine deutsche Biographie* (Leipzig, 1876), IV, he is listed as "berühmter Berg- und Hüttemann," and the official publication, already referred to, *Die königlich Sächsische Bergakademie zu Freiberg*, p. 8, lists him as one of the outstanding former teachers at the Academy. As the fiancé of Charpentier's daughter, Novalis frequently visited his home and no doubt discussed mathematics with him.

To supplement his formal lectures, Novalis received private instruction in mathematics from the French student Jean François Aubisson de Voisins (1769-1841); or, as Hiebel puts it: "When he found the lectures of the mathematics instructors too tedious, he sought the study of higher mathematics by a private tutor" (*Novalis*, Engl. version, p. 39). We obtain this information from a letter of Novalis to his father, dated at Freiberg September 1, 1798, in which he accounts for his expenditures: "D'Aubisson bin ich jetzt zwölf Wochen schuldig. Ich kann nicht gut ihm die sechs Wochen abziehn, da ich entfernt war, besonders, da er es nicht einmal prätendiert. Von ihm lern ich eigentlich Mathematik – und das Geld an Lempe ist weggeworfen. Ich lerne nichts bei ihm. Er gibt sich nicht die mindeste Mühe, seine Zuhörer wirklich weiterzubringen. Er liest äusserst unangenehm – läuft, was er kann und ist froh, wenn er uns sagen kann: ich habe gelesen" (IV, 237). Johann Friedrich Lempe (1757-1801) was professor of mathematics and physics at the Mining Academy from 1785 to 1801. D'Aubisson had studied mathematics at one of the French secondary schools that were the first in Europe to emphasize mathematics to the exclusion of some of the classical studies. He later gained renown as an engineer in France. Also, d'Aubisson came from the country of birth of modern chemistry and was eager to associate mathematics with this subject. Novalis jotted down the following note in his fragments: "D'Aubissons chemische Erläuterung der Buchstabenrechnung. Diese Zeichen schliessen nicht wie Zahlen ineinander, sondern man sieht noch in jeder Komposition der Elemente ihre Verhältnisse und die Methode der Komposition. Ils s'associent, mais ils ne se confondent pas"

(III, 351). Apparently d'Aubisson had explained to Novalis the use of letters in algebra with an illustration from chemistry. We shall use modern chemical notation in reproducing d'Aubisson's argument, although at that time a different notation was used. In the formula H_2SO_4 both the qualitative and quantitative composition of the formula is indicated. Similarly, an algebraic expression, say, $\sqrt{a^2 + b^2 + c^2}$, shows how the quantities a, b, and c have been composed, whereas the number 30 does not, as it stands, have to be necessarily regarded as the result of $\sqrt{3^2 + 4^2 + 5^2}$, even if $30 = \sqrt{3^2 + 4^2 + 5^2}$.

Most of Novalis' fragments on mathematics were written at Freiberg, although some of them show connections with his sojourn in Leipzig. The published portion of these fragments is collected under the general heading *Aus den Freiberger Studienheften und -blättern* (1798/99). It contains the "Mathematisches Heft. 23 Junius" (1798) (III, 17f.), "Mathematische Fragmente" (III, 20-23), "Arithmetica Universalis" (III, 23-25), "Aus den physikalischen Studienheften" (III, 26-45), and many other passages on mathematics. There are references to mathematics on almost every page of *Das allgemeine Brouillon* (III, 63-275). The collection *Fragmente der letzten Jahre* (1799/1800) (III, 283-353) contains the so-called "hymns to mathematics," written mainly at Weissenfels, Novalis' residence from May 12, 1799 to his death on March 25, 1801.

It is now possible to estimate the extent of Novalis' mathematical knowledge. We have seen that he studied mathematics at the University at Leipzig during his stay of a year and a half in that city, and for another year and a half at the Mining Academy at Freiberg. There can hardly be any doubt that in Leipzig he became acquainted with Hindenburg, the founder of the combinatorial school. At Freiberg he studied under Charpentier, and, being engaged to his daughter, had social contacts with him. He received additional private instruction in mathematics from d'Aubisson at Freiberg, and, above all, studied on his own. Persons who knew him testify that he was well versed in mathematics. His superior, District Inspector of Salt Mines August C. Just, stated after Novalis' death that the latter had already had "feine Vorkenntnisse" in mathematics before taking up study at Freiberg. Tieck wrote in his biography of Novalis (1815): "Seine Kenntnisse in der Mathematik sowie in den Künsten der Mechanik, vorzüglich aber in der Bergwerkskunde waren ausgezeichnet" (IV, 457). Most Novalis scholars agree that he was well versed in mathematics. It would seem that Novalis was familiar with most results of mathematics generally known at his time. His knowledge of calculus reflects the phase in the development of this branch of mathematics as it is laid down in

Euler's *Institutiones calculi differentialis* (1755), *Institutiones calculi integralis* (1768-1770), and in part as presented by Lagrange in his *Théorie des fonctions analytiques* (1797) (See also Section 4).

3. PHILOSOPHICAL SOURCES FOR NOVALIS' FRAGMENTS ON MATHEMATICS

Novalis' thought on mathematics shows points of contact with the works of various philosophers. We agree with Haering's viewpoint expressed in the chapter "Selbständigkeit und fremde Einflüsse" of his recent study of Novalis' philosophy (*op. cit.*, pp. 605-635), that "die vorgefasste Meinung und Legende, dass Novalis in allen seinen philosophischen Meditationen" reveals only "sklavische Übernahmen und unselbständige Reproduktionen Fichte-Hemsterhuisscher Gedanken" (p. 605), must be discarded. The influence of Plotinus, Baader, Böhme, Friedrich Schlegel, Ritter, Werner, Hülsen, Spinoza has been of secondary importance. "Unendlich viel wichtiger als alle diese Beeinflussungen sind daher für die besondere philosophische Haltung des Novalis, wie schon unsere Einzelausführungen unzweifelhaft ergaben, diejenigen durch *Fichte*, *Kant* und *Hemsterhuis* gewesen" (p. 618). In the more specific range of Novalis' thought on mathematics Haering's contention is also valid. We shall now consider the various points of contact between the works of such philosophers as Kant, Fichte, and Hemsterhuis and Novalis' fragments on mathematics separately.

Kant. Kant's relation to mathematics has been frequently discussed. Oskar Becker, for example, summarizes in his book *Mathematische Existenz* (Halle, 1927): "Es ist bekannt, dass Kant die beiden mathematischen Urdisziplinen Arithmetik und Geometrie den beiden Anschauungsformen Zeit und Raum zuordnet. Wie der reine Raum der Geometrie, so liegt die reine Zeit der Arithmetik zugrunde" (p. 213). Kant is convinced of the general and necessary validity of mathematical truths. However, this conception of mathematics has met with criticism in the light of modern geometrical considerations. "Wenn wirklich eine Anschauung a priori in seinem Sinn existiert, so kann sie nur eine einzige Form besitzen; es ist also auch nur eine Geometrie möglich, die zugleich in der empirischen Anschauung Bestätigung findet" (Voss, p. 94). Kant's theory of mathematical knowledge according to which only one, namely, Euclidean, geometry is possible, was refuted by the introduction of non-Euclidean geometries.

As a student at the University at Königsberg, Kant devoted himself, among other subjects, to mathematics. From 1755 to 1760 he lectured on this subject each semester (see Erich Adickes, *Kant als Naturforscher*, Berlin, 1924, I, 5). Yet, according to Adickes, his purely and strictly mathematical writings as contained in the *Lose Blätter aus dem Nachlass Kants* (ed. Ricke, 1889, 1895, 1898) are of little significance to mathematics proper. However, from a more general point of view, Kant's views on mathematics have been very influential; in fact, mathematics is one of the main pillars of his philosophy. Some of Novalis' fragments on mathematics are related to Kant's pronouncements on this subject in his *Kritik der reinen Vernunft* (1781), *Prolegomena zu einer jeden künftigen Metaphysik* (1783), and the *Metaphysische Anfangsgründe der Naturwissenschaft* (1786).

In the *Kritik der reinen Vernunft* (*Werke*, 12th ed., Leipzig: Meiner, 1922, I, hereafter abbreviated *KRV*), some of the basic concepts in the analysis of pure reason are illustrated with examples from mathematics. Mathematical theorems are proof for the existence of necessary and generally valid *a priori* judgments (*KRV*, 50). Kant makes the famous distinction between analytic (or explicative) judgments, in which the predicate is already tacitly contained in the subject, and synthetic (or ampliative) judgments, in which the predicate lies entirely outside the subject (*KRV*, 55). Within the framework of this distinction, Kant makes another important observation on the nature of mathematics: "Mathematische Urteile sind insgesamt synthetisch" (*KRV*, 59). Mathematical judgments are synthetic, and not analytic, or tautological, or identical, as Leibniz, d'Alembert, and Goethe held. Thus mathematical judgments are (1) *a priori*, (2) synthetic. But since to Kant empirical judgments are synthetic ("Erfahrungsurteile als solche sind insgesamt synthetisch," *KRV*, 56), someone may be tempted to reverse the orientation of the implication and think that mathematical judgments are empirical. To prevent such possible misconception, Kant divests mathematical judgments of all empirical connotations by restricting his argument to pure mathematics: "...muss eigentlich bemerkt werden, dass eigentliche mathematische Sätze jederzeit Urteile a priori und nicht empirisch sind, weil sie Notwendigkeit bei sich führen, welche aus Erfahrung nicht abgenommen werden kann. Will man aber dieses nicht einräumen, wohlan, so schränke ich meinen Satz auf die reine Mathematik ein, deren Begriff es schon mit sich bringt, dass sie nicht empirische, sondern bloss reine Erkenntnis a priori enthalte" (*KRV*, 60). The basic problem of pure reason in Kant's *KRV* is formulated as follows: "Wie sind synthetische Urteile a priori möglich?" (How are a priori synthetic judgments possible?) (*KRV*, 63). Metaphysics cannot be said to exist, and therefore there is reason to doubt that it is possible at all. However, pure mathematics and pure physics exist, hence we may ask whether they are possible. Now we already know that mathematics, and also physics (*KRV*, 64), contains synthetic a priori judgments. Therefore, the pivotal problem of pure reason, *i.e.*, whether a priori synthetic judgments are possible, involves also the questions: "Wie ist reine Mathematik möglich?" (How is pure mathematics possible?) and "Wie ist reine Naturwissenschaft möglich?" (John Watson translates: How is pure physics possible?) (for this English version, see Benjamin Rand's anthology *Modern Classical Philosophers*, 3rd ed., Boston, etc., 1936, pp. 366 & 379).

Novalis takes up Kant's question whether synthetic a priori judgments are possible and adds other variants to it: "Kants Frage: Sind synthetische Urteile a priori möglich, lässt sich auf mannigfaltige Weise spezifischer ausdrücken. Z.B.

Ist die Philosophie eine Kunst (eine Dogmatik, Wissenschaft)?
Gibt es eine Erfindungskunst ohne Data, eine absolute Erfindungskunst?
Lassen sich Krankheiten nach Belieben machen etc.?
Lassen sich Verse nach Regeln und ein Wahnwitz nach Grundsätzen denken?
Ist ein *perpetuum mobile* möglich etc.?
Ist ein Genie möglich – lässt sich ein Genie definieren?
Lässt sich der Zirkel quadrieren?
Ist Magie möglich?
Lässt sich Gott, Freiheit und Unsterblichkeit demonstrieren?
Gibt es eine Rechnung des Unendlichen? etc." (III, 230f.)

At first glance we seem to have here a haphazard agglomeration of questions, but on closer examination they turn out to be valid variants of Kant's original question within Novalis' thought. Kant states in the *KRV* that metaphysics is not a science, and that it has always suffered from an excess of dogma. Novalis wonders whether, more generally, philosophy is an art, dogma, or a science. He further inquires: Is there an art of invention without data, an absolute art of invention? This is equivalent to asking whether synthetic *a priori* judgments are possible. Synthetic means nonanalytic, this accounts for Novalis' expression "Erfindungskunst"; *a priori* implies non-empirical, hence Novalis states "without data," *i.e.*, without empirical data. In his *Ars combinatoria* Leibniz had hoped to obtain new truths through various combinations of ideas and data. Novalis wonders whether such an art is possible without data. Novalis further inquires whether "a genius is possible?" What is the relation of genius to "synthetic?" Simon shows that Novalis regarded the synthetic function as an ideal function, and that the latter designated it by "genial" (Simon, p. 24). Hamburger takes up Simon's argument and declares that Novalis' variants of

Kant's question show "dass Synthesis für ihn die Bedeutung eines schöpferischen Prinzips gewinnt, weil er die Frage nach der Möglichkeit synthetischer Urteile in eine Reihe stellt mit der Frage nach der Möglichkeit des Genies und der Magie" (Hamburger, p. 123). Thus she arrives, again in the footsteps of Simon, at a partial explanation of Novalis' hymns to mathematics. Novalis held that "synthetische Urteile sind genialische, nicht antinomische, einseitige Urteile" (III, 180). The attribute of genius is to produce synthetic knowledge. For this reason Novalis asks whether genius is possible. Wherever empirical limitations or physical boundaries are imposed, Novalis wonders whether these limitations may be overcome. In this connection he considers such problems: Is magic possible? Is a perpetual mobile possible? etc. (see also *Das allgemeine Brouillon*, Nr. 1036, III, 259). Novalis also asks: Can (the existence of) God, freedom, and immortality be demonstrated? Kant had stated in his *KRV*, p. 52: "Die unvermeidlichen Aufgaben der reinen Vernunft sind Gott, Freiheit und Unsterblichkeit." But since they can neither be demonstrated nor disproved, Kant introduced them as postulates of practical reason in his *Kritik der praktischen Vernunft*.

Another point of contact between Kant's and Novalis' conception of mathematics is found in the former's table of categories. This table appears in *KRV*, p. 130, as follows:

1 *Quantität*		(We may interpret the first two categories mathematically as follows:)
Einheit	Unity	one element
Vielheit	Plurality	some elements
Allheit	Totality	all elements
2 *Qualität*		
Realität	Reality	there exists
Negation	Negation	there does not exist
Limitation	Limitation	there exist some
3 *Relation*		
der Inhärenz und Subsistenz (substantia et accidens)		Inherence and Subsistence
der Causalität und Dependenz (Ursache und Wirkung)		Causality and Dependence (cause and effect)
der Gemeinschaft (Wechselwirkung zwischen dem Handelnden und Leidenden)		Community (reciprocity between the active and the passive)
4 *Modalität*		
Möglichkeit – Unmöglichkeit		Possibility – Impossibility
Dasein – Nichtsein		Existence – Non-Existence
Notwendigkeit – Zufälligkeit		Necessity – Contingency

Kant calls quality and quantity *mathematical* categories; relation and modality, *dynamical* (*KRV*, 133). Novalis comments: "Wir können die Einteilung in *mathematische*, die sich auf die Kausalität des Begreifens, die Anschauung, und in *dynamische*, die sich auf die Kausalität des Fühlens gründen, beibehalten" (II, 105). Novalis designates quantity as "die Form der Anschauung," quality as "die Form des Begriffs," relations as "die Form des Gefühls," and modality as "die Form der Empfindung," so that "die *mathematischen* Kategorien sind die Formen der Anschauung und die Formen des Begriffs" (II, 106). In the eighteenth century such mathematicians as Euler defined mathematics as limited to quantity, although in their actual mathematical work they transcended this category. Kant formally prepares the ground for an extension of mathematics from the category of quantity to the category of quality by classifying these two categories as mathematical. Similarly, Novalis attempted to extend the validity of mathematics beyond the category of quantity into the ranges of the other three categories in Kant's system. The first step in this process was to eliminate the barrier between quality and quantity. Hence we find that Novalis was preoccupied with "Übersetzung der Qualität und Quantität, und umgekehrt" (III, 248). Novalis wonders: "Soll aller Unterschied nur quantitativ sein? Selbst zwischen Gott und mir? Absolutierung der Mathematik" (III, 23). Mathematics is to be absolutized and generalized, *i.e.*, extended from quantity to quality, and beyond that into the dynamical categories of relation and modality. "Wenn jene erste die quantitative, die zweite die qualitative Mathematik ist, so ist die dritte die relative Mathematik – die in vier Gliedersystemen und einem Universalsystem erscheint. (Kategorien, Fichtes Wissenschaftslehre)" (III, 22). Of this pure, universal mathematics Novalis then says: "Reine Mathematik hat nichts mit Grösse zu tun. Sie ist blosse Bezeichnungslehre – mechanisch gewordener, in Verhältnissen geordneter Gedankenoperationen" (III, 325). Thus Novalis boldly transgresses the boundaries of Kant's categories and uses them in extended form in his own thought. Applying the categories to geometry, Novalis finds in this branch of mathematics "allgemeine Gesetze der Ähnlichkeit (Qualität), Gleichheit (Quantität) und der Verhältnisse (Relation)..." (III, 29).

Kant's references to mathematics in his transcendental aesthetic (*KRV*, 75-105) are further developed by Novalis. Kant starts out with a definition of intuition (Anschauung). Intuition is knowledge (Erkenntnis) which is in immediate relation to objects ("sich auf Gegenstände unmittelbar bezieht," *KRV*, 75) (for English formulations see Norman Kemp Smith, *A Commentary to Kant's Critique of Pure Reason*, 2nd ed., London, 1930, p. 79). The faculty of receiving representations (Vorstellungen) according to the manner in which we are affected by objects, is called sensibility (Sinnlichkeit) (*KRV*, 75) (see also Max Müller, *I. Kant's Critique of Pure Reason*, transl. into English, New York, p. 15). Sensibility supplies us with intuitions. Time and space are introduced as the two forms of intuition. Time is the form of the inward sense, of the intuition of our self (*KRV*, 89). Space, as the pure form of outward intuition, is limited to outward phenomena. Time and space are, according to Kant, the logical foundations of mathematics. "Geometrie liegt die reine Anschauung des Raumes zum Grunde. Arithmetik bringt selbst ihre Zahlbegriffe durch sukzessive Hinzusetzung der Einheiten in der Zeit zustande" (*Prolegomena zu einer jeden künftigen Metaphysik, Werke*, 12th ed., III, Section 10). Novalis observes in this context: "Nach Kant bezieht sich reine Mathematik und Naturwissenschaft auf die Formen der äusseren Sinnlichkeit. Welche Wissenschaft bezieht sich denn auf die Formen der inneren Sinnlichkeit? – Gibt es eine aussersinnliche Erkenntnis? Ist noch ein anderer Weg offen, aus sich selbst herauszugehen und zu anderen Wesen zu gelangen oder von ihnen affiziert zu werden?" (II, 304). The science of inward sensibility is probably music. Novalis associates music with arithmetic and algebra. A very likely chain of associations in Novalis' mind is: music – arithmetic – inward sense – inward sensibility (see Chapter IV, section "Mathematics and Music"). After considering the two possibilities of outward and inward sensibility, Novalis logically asks the next question: Is there such a thing as extra-sensory knowledge? Is there another road which will lead us to other beings, or which will lead other beings to us? As in the case of Kant's categories, Novalis quickly conquers the domain of Kant's arguments, and then pushes further into the unknown. Since the first element in the sequence "outward sensation, inward sensation, extra-sensory perception" was mathematics, and the second element appears to be mathematized inward sensibility as revealed in music, Novalis' next step would be to mathematize extra-sensory perception. Thus Novalis was led to "magische Mathematik" (See Chapter IV, Section "Mathematics and Magic").

Novalis owned a copy of Kant's *Metaphysische Anfangsgründe der Naturwissenschaft* (Riga, 1786; 2. Auflage, 1787) (*Werke*, 12th ed., VII, hereafter abbreviated *MAN*), and used some of the ideas set forth in this work as points of departure for his mathematical thought. A major hypothesis of the *MAN* is that natural sciences may be regarded as sciences only insofar as they contain mathematics: "Ich behaupte aber, dass in jeder besonderen Naturlehre nur so viel eigentliche Wissenschaft angetroffen werden könne, als darin Mathematik anzutreffen ist" (*MAN*, 193). The reason for this assertion was already given in the *KRV* and in the *Prolegomena* (33), where he states that mathematical knowledge is of apodictic certainty and absolute necessity. Also, mathematical knowledge is obtained *a priori*. "Nun heisst etwas a priori erkennen, es aus seiner blossen Möglichkeit zu erkennen" (*MAN*, 193) (For this reason Kant asks in the *KRV* whether mathematics is possible, although it actually exists). "Also wird, um die Möglichkeit bestimmter Naturdinge, mithin um diese a priori zu erkennen, noch erfordert, dass die dem Begriffe korrespondierende Anschauung a priori gegeben werde, d. i., dass der Begriff konstruiert werde. Nun ist die Vernunfterkenntnis durch Konstruktion der Begriffe mathematisch" (*MAN*, 193). Similarly, Kant states in the *Prolegomena*, p. 18: "Das Wesentliche und Unterscheidende der reinen mathematischen Erkenntnis a priori ist, dass sie durchaus nicht aus Begriffen, sondern jederzeit nur durch die Konstruktion dieser Begriffe vor sich gehen muss." In this context, Novalis observes in his "Arithmetica universalis": "Die Frage nach der Möglichkeit der Mathematik zerfällt in zwei Teile – 1. Ist sie möglich? 2. Wie ist sie möglich? (Kants Verfahren mit der Metaphysik – die ihm mit der Philosophie synonym ist. Seine berühmte Frage) (Sie ist die Frage nach der Möglichkeit und Konstruktionsmethode des philosophischen Genies). Grundproblem der Mathematik: Gibt es ein mathematisches (Leben) Genie? Wie ist es möglich? Erstere Auflösung liefert den Satz – die andere den Beweis, die Konstruktionsmethode dazu)" (III, 25). Questions 1 and 2 refer to the fundamental question in the *KRV*: how are *a priori* synthetic judgments possible? The question about "Genie" as another variant of Kant's question was already discussed in the preceding. Novalis now equates the question about the possibility of genius with the question about the possibility of constructing mathematical concepts.

Fichte, Baader, Hemsterhuis, and others. The general impact of Fichte on Novalis is discussed by Haering (pp. 618-626). He is convinced that Novalis read, immediately upon publication, most of Fichte's works published within the poet's lifetime. Novalis specifically refers to the *Grundlage der gesamten Wissenschaftslehre* (1794/95) (IV, 207; II, 159).

While Fichte seldom deals with mathematics explicitly, there is in his works a mathematicity of a general nature that appealed to Novalis. Like Descartes and Spinoza, Fichte attempts to axiomatize his system of philosophy (cf. Ludwig Fischer, *Die Grundlagen der Philosophie und Mathematik*, Leipzig, 1933, p. 8). Fichte begins with a fundamental concept, the Ego (Ich), and three axioms: the principle of identity, the principle of contradiction, and the principle of sufficient reason, or "thesis, antithesis, synthesis." The concept of Ego yields in conjunction with each of the three axioms successively the propositions: Ich bin Ich (Ego is Ego); Ich bin Nicht-Ich (Ego is Non-Ego); Ich bin zum Teil Nicht-Ich (I am in part Non-Ego), or, Nicht-Ich ist zum Teil Ich (Non-Ego is in part Ego) (see *Grundlage der gesamten Wissenschaftslehre*, Fichte's *Werke*, Leipzig: Meiner, 1922, I, 285-519). The philosophy Fichte deduces from his premises is reflected in numerous passages of Novalis' *Philosophische Studien* (1795/97) (II, 103-308). For example, Novalis remarks: "Alle Wissenschaften ruhen auf der einfachen Wissenschaft, dem einfachen, synthetisierenden Satze – Ich" (III, 28). All sciences are based on the Ego. But since all sciences are to be mathematized, and, moreover, Fichte's "Wissenschaftslehre" (science of knowledge) is based on the Ego, Novalis concludes: "Die Wissenschaftslehre muss die Mathematik begründen" (II, 269). Another influence of Fichte on Novalis' fragments on mathematics is pointed out by Dietrich Mahnke in his book *Unendliche Sphäre und Allmittelpunkt*, p. 2, which we briefly mentioned in the introductory chapter. He traces the concept of sphere in Novalis' notes on "Sphäroidik" or mystical geometry partially to Fichte's "Ich-Sphären."

Benedikt Franz Xaver von Baader (1765-1841), to whom Novalis refers with respect and enthusiasm (II, 324; IV, 241), wrote an essay entitled *Über das pythagoräische Quadrat oder die vier Weltgegenden* (1798). Novalis read this essay and described it as "nichts wie derbe, gediegene Poesie" (IV, 261). It is a mystical essay with vague mathematical associations (see David Baumgart, *Franz von Baader und die philosophische Romantik*, Halle, 1927, p. 202). In his *Beiträge zur Elementarphysiologie* (1797) Baader exalts enthusiasm as a force in the advancement of knowledge at the expense of the mathematical approach. Novalis fused enthusiasm and mathematics: "Der echte Mathematiker ist Enthusiast per se" (III, 296). In his *Elementarphysiologie* Baader also demanded a "lebendige, dynamische Arithmetik" instead of the "tote begriffslose Addition und Subtraktion" (see Baader, *Sämtliche Werke*, Leipzig, 1852-57, III, 236). Similarly, Novalis sought to widen the domain of mathematics from quantity and quality to the dynamical categories of relation and modality.

We have already dealt with Hemsterhuis' influence on Novalis' mathematical fragments in Section 2 of this chapter. Among other philosophers whose works stimulated Novalis' thought on mathematics are Eckartshausen (1752-1803) (See Chapter I, Section 3), Pascal's *Pensées*, and Spinoza. From the *Encyclopédie* (Paris, 1751-1772) Novalis excerpted the following passage: "L'arithmétique est l'art de trouver d'une maniére abrégée l'expression d'un rapport unique, qui résulte de la comparaison de pluseurs autres. Les différentes manières de comparer ces rapports donnent les différentes règles de l'arithmétique. Les formules algébraiques sont des calculs arithmétiques indiqués."

4. MATHEMATICAL SOURCES FOR NOVALIS' FRAGMENTS ON MATHEMATICS

After Novalis' death his brother Karl compiled a list of books found in Novalis' library. This "Verzeichnis der Bücher, so sich auf der Stube des Salinenassessors von Hardenberg befinden" (IV, 476-481) lists several mathematical texts, or books closely related in subject matter. They are listed below, preceded by the numbers in Karl's list:

46. Abel Burja, *Mathematische Wissenschaften*. [I was unable to trace this book].
54. Pierre Simon de Laplace, *Darstellung des Weltsystems*. Aus dem Französischen von J. K. F. Hauff (Frankfurt, 1797-98). 2 Bände.
95. Johann Heinrich Erich Rehbein, *Versuch einer neuen Grundlegung der Geometrie* (Göttingen, 1795).
108. Johann Georg Büsch, *Versuch einer Mathematik zum Nutzen und Vergnügen des bürgerlichen Lebens*. 4. Auflage (Hamburg, 1798). 2 Abteilungen.
126. Karl Friedrich Hindenburg, *Novi systematis permutationum, combinationum etc. primae liniae* (Leipzig, 1781).
127. Konrad Dietrich Martin Stahl, *Anfangsgründe der Zahlenarithmetik und Buchstabenrechnung, zum Gebrauch bei Vorlesungen* (Jena, 1797).
128. J. L. Lagrange, *Theorie der analytischen Funktionen, in welcher die Grundsätze der Differentialrechnung vorgetragen werden*. Aus dem Französischen von Gruson (Berlin, 1798). 2 Bände.
129. Abel Burja, *Der selbstlernende Algebraist oder Anweisung zur ganzen Rechenkunst* (Berlin, 1786). 2 Bände.
130. Abraham Gotthold Kästner, *Anfangsgründe der Analysis des Unendlichen* (Göttingen, 1760; 3. Auflage, 1799).
131. Karl Friedrich Hindenburg, *Der polynomische Lehrsatz*. Sammlungen kombinatorisch-analytischer Abhandlungen, Band 1 (Leipzig, 1796).
132. Heinrich August Töpfer, *Kombinatorische Analytik und Theorie der Dimensionszeichen, in Parallele gestellt* (Leipzig, 1793).
133. Georg v. Vega, *Logarithmisch-trigonometrische Tafeln* (Leipzig, 1793; 2. Auflage, 1800).

A number of other books of more general content along scientific and philosophical lines in this list have bearing on mathematics. The mere fact that Novalis was in possession of these books does not, of course, imply that he used any or all of them. However, his fragments on mathematics reveal at least a general acquaintance with them in most cases, a more intimate acquaintance with the books by Hindenburg and Töpfer, as we have already shown in Section 2 of this chapter. Some of the authors are specifically mentioned in the "Materialien" for Novalis' projected "Arithmetica Universalis" (III, 23). Despite this proximity in subject matter, a detailed comparison of these books with Novalis' fragments on mathematics fails to turn any of the latter into excerpts of the former, and thus fails to support frequently made claims that Novalis' fragments utterly lack originality.

We shall briefly point out some peculiar aspects of the more important of these books with a view to elucidating Novalis' fragments on mathematics. From the viewpoint of mathematics proper, the most important text in Novalis' possession is Lagrange's *Théorie des fonctions analytiques*, first published in 1797. Joseph Louis Lagrange (1736-1813) was professor of mathematics at the Royal Artillery School at Turin before his twenty-year long association with the Academy of Science in Berlin. In his *Théorie des fonctions analytiques*, and also in his *Leçons sur le calcul des fonctions* (1801), he had attempted to "give a solid foundation to the calculus by reducing it to algebra" (Struik, II, 191). The derivatives $f'(x), f''(x)$, etc. are defined by him as the coefficients $h, \frac{h^2}{2}, \ldots \frac{h^n}{n!}$ in the Taylor expansion of $f(x-h)$ in terms of h. He obtained the Taylor series itself by a purely algebraic process that turned out to be unsatisfactory (Struik, II, 191). Lagrange's method and aims are succinctly summed up in the subtitle of his book, which reads: (*Théorie des fonctions analytiques*) "contenant les principes du calcul différentiel, dégagés de toute considération d'infiniment petits, d'évanouissans, de limites et de fluxions, et réduits à l'analyse algébrique des quantités finies (see Nouvelle edition, Paris, 1813). Lagrange criticises his predecessors Leibniz, Bernoulli, l'Hospital, Euler, and d'Alembert for their indiscriminate use of infinitesimals and the shaky foundations of their calculus. His own attempt to develop calculus without using the concepts of "vanishing quantities" (*i.e.*, infinitesimal quantities), "fluxions" (*i.e.*, derivatives), and limits proved to be just as shaky as the foundations of his predecessors. Nevertheless Lagrange's texts were widely used before the appearance of Cauchy's *Cours d'Analyse de l'École Royale Polytechnique* in 1821, which presented, for the first time, satisfactory definitions of the concepts of limit, continuity, and derivative. Thus Novalis' numerous queries and suggestions on the nature of infinitesimal calculus reflect not only the romanticist's desire to widen and deepen the ranges of formal mathematics for his own world view, but also the general confusion about the foundations of calculus and other branches of mathematics manifested by the works of the greatest mathematicians of the time.

Next in importance among mathematical texts owned by Novalis is Kästner's *Anfangsgründe der Analysis des Unendlichen*, first published in 1760. Kästner, whom Gauss teasingly called the first poet among mathematicians and the first mathematician among poets, steps boldly from the realm of mathematics into the region of poetry if it is necessary to deal with the inexplicable (cf. Cajori, p. 435). Before presenting his theories, he intoxicates himself and the reader with the enigmatic nature of the concept of infinity:

Geheimnisse müssen doch etwas sehr reizendes für den menschlichen Verstand sein, weil man selbst in derjenigen Wissenschaft dergleichen zu haben gesucht hat, die seit Tausenden von Jahren, ihrer Deutlichkeit und augenscheinlichen Überzeugung wegen berühmt gewesen ist. Man sieht ohne mein Erinnern, dass ich die Lehre vom Unendlichen in der Mathematik meine, wie sie von vielen Schriftstellern, selbst solchen die das Reich der Wissenschaften dadurch erweitert haben, vorgetragen wird. Grössen, die unterschieden sind und doch als gleich angesehen werden; unendlich grosse Dinge die in Vergleichung mit anderen nichts, und unendlich kleine die in Vergleichung mit anderen unendlich gross sind; krumme Linien, die aus geraden Teilchen bestehen, welche gerade Teilchen man nach Gefallen wieder krümmt wie man will, und unzählig andere solche Sätze die wider die ersten Gründe aller menschlichen Erkenntnis anzustossen scheinen, sollen von den Schülern der Mathematik als die erhabensten Lehren ehrfurchtsvoll angenommen werden. Könnte Aberglauben was mehr von seinen Anbetern fordern, wenn er nach Hallers Ausdrucke: mit Rauch die schimmernden Gewölber füllt?

(Kästner, *Anfangsgründe*, p. iii).

Then Kästner, professor of mathematics at the University at Göttingen, and Gauss' teacher, continues: "Wie sich der kühne Ausdruck eines Dichters von dem vielleicht logisch richtigern, aber trockenen Vortrage unterscheidet, so ist ohngefähr die Rechnung des Unendlichen von den Beweisen der Alten unterschieden: auch hat das feste Land sie zuerst von einem Geiste gelernt, bei dem sich der Witz des Dichters, die Einsicht des Philosophen, die Gründlichkeit des Geometers und die Belesenheit des Polyhistors vereinigten" (Kästner, p. iv; he obviously refers to Leibniz). Thus Kästner juxtaposes the rigor of ancient geometry with the looseness of the calculus of his own age. Ancient geometry had dealt mainly with finite magnitudes. Modern calculus rests on the fundamental concepts of infinity and infinitesimals. Of the latter two, however, eighteenth-century mathematicians still had a dim and muddled conception. In the above passages Kästner points out some of the seeming paradoxes associated with the concepts. The infinite and infinitesimal, as upper and lower limits of expansion, spacial and temporal, physical and imaginary, were of particular interest to the early German Romanticists, notably Novalis and Friedrich Schlegel.

Both linked these concepts with mathematics. Even Kästner feels that the poetic boldness of the calculus based on these concepts compensates its lack of rigor.

Kästner actually denies the existence of infinitely large and small quantities. To determine the differential, Kästner considers the function Z of the independent variable z. If z is given an increment e, Z will become $Z + E$. "If now e is indefinitely diminished, the limit which the ratio $E : e$ approaches indefinitely, is called the ratio of the differentials of Z and z, and the infinitely small quantities e and E are called the differentials of z and Z" (Kästner, p. 10, as translated by Boyer, *op. cit.*, p. 250). Thus Kästner does not distinguish between increments and differentials, yet he cannot avoid the use of infinitely small quantities in his discussion, despite his denial of their existence (cf. Boyer, p. 250 and Cantor, IV, 642). A mathematician will see how far removed Kästner was from a precise and satisfactory definition of the derivative and differential and realize the effect of arguments based on such insufficient definition on Novalis' mind.

Abel Burja's *Der selbstlernende Algebraist*, another text Novalis owned, is interesting and instructive as it illuminates eighteenth-century groping for a foundation of calculus. In this book an attempt is made to pass over from the calculus of finite differences to differential calculus. A first difference is defined (II, 79) as

$$\Delta z = \Delta (xy) = y\Delta x + x\Delta y + \Delta x \Delta y,$$

where $z = xy$
the second difference as

$$\Delta^2 z = 2\Delta x \Delta y + y\Delta^2 x + x\Delta^2 y + 2\Delta x \Delta^2 y + 2\Delta y \Delta^2 x + \Delta^2 x \Delta y$$

Then he introduces the operator Σ as the inverse of the Δ operator (II, 100, 101), so that

$$\Sigma (x\Delta y + y\Delta x + \Delta x \Delta y) = xy$$

i. e. $$\Sigma \{\Delta (xy)\} = xy.$$

A transition to differential calculus is made as follows. We already obtained

(1) $$\Delta z = y \Delta x + x\Delta y + \Delta x \Delta y,$$

where $$z = xy$$

Burja then explains: "Sind nun Δx und Δy sehr klein in Vergleichung mit x und y, so hat man beinahe

(2) $$\Delta z = y\Delta x + x\Delta y.“$$

The expression (1) is called "vollständige Differenz," (2) is called "unvollständige Differenz" or "Differential" (II, 141). Similarly, a transition is made from the operator Σ to $\int$.

Burja's book *Der selbstlernende Algebraist* reveals once more the primitive conception of the basis of calculus in the late eighteenth century. Yet, as a professor of mathematics at the Academie militaire at Berlin, he must be regarded as a full-fledged mathematician of his time. His algebra for self-study was widely used, especially among non-professional mathematicians. It is, therefore, of extreme importance to our evaluation of Novalis' fragments on mathematics.

Novalis' fragments on mathematics contain casual references to the following mathematicians or physicists: Klügel, Newton, Bezout, Vieth, Mönch, Stahl, Kästner, Schulz, and others (for a few details see Hamburger, p. 117).

Although Novalis' published fragments refer only once to Euler (III, 67; Euler's views on the nature of light), his fragments on mathematics indicate that he was directly or indirectly acquainted with Euler's *Institutiones Calculi Differentialis* (Auctore Leonardo Eulero. Impensis Academiae Imperialis Scientiarum Petropolitanae, 1755; especially: Caput III: De infinitis atque infinite paruis, pp. 70-97), in particular, with Chapter III on infinity. Novalis or his teachers no doubt used also the German translation of this work by J. A. Ch. Michelsen, professor of mathematics and physics at the Berlinisches Gymnasium (Leonhard Eulers *Vollständige Anleitung zur Differential-Rechnung*. Aus dem Lat. übersetzt von Johann Andreas Christian Michelsen, Berlin & Libau, 1790, 3 Teile; especially 3. Kapitel: Von dem Unendlichen und dem unendlich Kleinen, pp. 71-100). In the preface to his *Institutiones Calculi Differentialis* Euler defines differential calculus as the method of determining the ratio between vanishing increments of the variables of a function:

Und auf diese Art sind wir zu der Definition des Differential-Calcüls gelangt, welcher nichts anderes ist, als die Methode, das Verhältnis der verschwindenden Incremente zu bestimmen, welche die Funktionen veränderlicher Grössen bekommen, wenn die veränderliche Grösse, wovon sie Funktionen sind, um ein verschwindendes Increment vermehrt worden. Dass diese Erklärung die Natur des Differential-Calcüls ausdrucke, ja sogar erschöpfe, wird jeder einsehen, der in diesem Teile der höheren Mathematik kein gänzlicher Fremdling ist. Es beschäftigt sich also die Differentialrechnung nicht sowohl mit diesen Incrementen selbst, denn diese sind Nullen; sondern vielmehr mit der Erforschung des Verhältnisses, welches sie zueinander haben: und da sich diese Verhältnisse durch endliche Grössen ausdrucken lassen, so muss man auch eigentlich sagen, dass die Differential-Rechnung endliche Grössen zum eigentlichen Gegenstande habe.

(Michelsen's transl., pp. liii-liv).

Cantor summarizes Euler's position in the development of calculus as follows: "Er entfernt sich von Leibniz, indem er von dem Unendlichkleinen nichts wissen will, er nimmt auch nicht mit Berkeley einander aufhebende Irrtümer an, er verschmäht Newtons Grenzwerte, er sieht in den Differentialen wirkliche Nullen, in den Differentialquotienten Brüche mit Nullen im Zähler und Nenner, welche aber gleichwohl einen endlichen Wert besitzen" (Cantor, III, 724). Joseph Ehrenfried Hofmann also declares that Euler's book "ist im Grundlegenden (die Differentiale werden als Nullen erklärt) unbefriedigend" (*Geschichte der Mathematik. 3 Teil: Von den Auseinandersetzungen um den Calculus bis zur französischen Revolution*, Berlin, 1957, p. 59; this volume is extremely enlightening with regard to the background of Novalis' fragments on mathematics). Euler's *Institutiones Calculi Differentialis*, the most important and influential study of differential calculus in the eighteenth century, reveals once again the fluctuating foundation of this subject at that time and the many points of departure, especially with regard to infinity and infinitesimals, for Novalis' fragments. The latter will be discussed in Section 4 ("Analysis") of the next chapter.

CHAPTER III

NOVALIS' FRAGMENTS ON MATHEMATICS, PART ONE
MATHEMATICS DISCUSSED PHILOSOPHICALLY

> Hardenbergs Fragmente über die Mathematik enthüllen die letzte Absicht seines Denkens und seiner Wissenschaft (p. 214).
>
> EDGAR HEDERER, 1949

1. BASIC CONCEPTS

Novalis gave much thought to mathematical method. He realized that if in a mathematical system certain rules were followed consistently and persistently enough, more and more results could be obtained. The mere realization of this did not gratify his intellectual curiosity. He explored such basic mathematical concepts as definition, axiom, proof, and theorem for their validity and possible extension to other fields of knowledge.

In this chapter we shall see how he enlisted the critical apparatus of fields of knowledge other than mathematics to elucidate and settle in his own mind the conceptual foundation of mathematics. In the next chapter we shall examine his employment of mathematical distinctions in branches of knowledge outside the domain of mathematics proper and the physical sciences.

In modern mathematics a distinction is sometimes made between *object* and *syntax* language. Mathematical symbols and formulae and their various combinations are in the first category; explanatory verbal remarks, in the latter. Object language is circumscribed by definition; syntax language is used to introduce and elucidate object language, and is then, if possible, discarded, because it smuggles in various nonmathematical, and hence disturbing and irrelevant, connotations. In such branches of mathematics as modern algebra and symbolic logic, attempts are being made to reduce all syntax language to object language, or, at least, to introduce the latter with a minimum of the former. For example, the expression "there exists" is replaced by the symbol $\exists$. This symbol is to prevent the student from obscuring the mathematical arguments, in a spontaneous overflow of emotions, or uninhibited lyrical response, by discoursing along the lines of "to be or not to be," or in terms of some metaphysical concept of existence, in the course of which the original "question" may elude him. P. Rosenbloom succinctly distills our distinction: "We use the object language to talk *within* the science and the syntax language to talk *about* the science" (*The Elements of Mathematical Logic*, New York, 1950, p. iii). Novalis and his contemporaries talked more about mathematics than within it. Euler, for example, frequently dissertates broadly (the modern mathematician would be tempted to say: loosely) on his subject, and does not hesitate to use such words as "mysterious," or to make an occasional prophecy. In the third chapter of his *Institutiones Calculi Differentialis*, a work already mentioned in the preceding chapter, he claims distinction between zeros of various orders and predicts that henceforth there should be no doubt about the subject. However, this distinction soon proved erroneous. At the other extreme, the modern mathematician diligently and laboriously weeds out all traces of human effort and toil until he finally obtains an ethereal structure so impersonal and objective that one cannot possibly tell, nor does one desire to know, who obtained the result. Yet the structure is so lucid and compelling that each individual has the vague sensation that he may have composed it himself a long time ago.

If we bear this distinction in mind, we will be better able to appreciate Novalis' more impulsive and extemporaneous utterances.

Novalis enunciates that the essence of mathematics resides in its method: "Die mathematische Methode ist das Wesen der Mathematik. Wer die Methode ganz versteht, ist Mathematiker" (III, 255). He who has completely grasped mathematical method is a real mathematician, and not the one that knows all results but cannot deduce them. He continues: "Sie ist als die wissenschaftliche Methode überhaupt höchst interessant und gibt vielleicht das richtigste Muster zur Einteilung des Erkenntnis- und Erfahrungsvermögens her" (III, 256). Moreover, mathematical method is perhaps the best tool to obtain knowledge and assimilate experience. This enunciation of Novalis' fundamental belief prepares us for his observations on more specific mathematical concepts.

Definition. A mathematical system is usually initiated by definitions, even if the elements of the system are, by definition, undefined. Novalis digs deeper and begins with a definition of definition: "Definitionen sind äussere (Merkmalsverzeichnungen) oder innere (Elementenverzeichnungen) oder gemischte. Es sind Konstruktionsformeln" (III, 20). A definition may be external or internal, or mixed. External definitions are descriptive labels, internal definitions are prescriptive within the system of elements. He continues: "Indirekte Definitionen sind Rezepte. Zu den Rezepten gehören die Experimentalvorschriften oder Beschreibungen (Positive und negative Definitionen)" (III, 20). Definitions are construction formulae or recipes. Novalis distinguishes between

positive and negative definitions. By the former he means defining
an object in terms of what it is; by the latter, in terms of what it is
not. The importance of adequate definitions is realized by Novalis
when he says: "Bessere Thesen (Definitionen) würden eine Menge
Sätze überflüssig machen" (III, 20). Better definitions would
render many theorems or propositions superfluous. The validity of
this assertion is demonstrated by the modern streamlining of mathematics. Some of Euclid's definitions, *e.g.*, that a point is that which
has no part, have been eliminated as having no effect on the system,
i.e., as not disturbing its consistency pattern, or as useless in formal
proofs of theorems. Novalis also reflects on the problem of the
relative priority of definitions and the results deduced from them.
"Aber wie erfahren wir denn, was eine Theorie ist? Es muss die
Lehre von den Gesetzen eines Dinges sein. Den Anfang muss die
Definition des Dinges machen. Aber Definition ohne Gesetze? wie
ist die anticipando möglich?" (II, 203). There is some doubt
in Novalis' mind as to the actual order of precedence of definition
and theory. Do we really start out with arbitrary definitions in a
mathematical system, or do we already have the results of the
theory in mind and then fit the definitions to the theory? Logically,
definition, *i.e.*, the statement of *first* principles, comes first, but
actually the historical development of mathematics shows numerous
instances where a result was first obtained intuitively or empirically,
and then placed on a substructure of definitions and axioms. One
only need to consider the many definitions of number that have
been offered at the various stages of the development of mathematics.
Novalis further comments on definition: "Eine Definition ist ein
realer oder generierender Name. Ein gewöhnlicher Namen ist nur
eine Nota... Die reale Definition ist ein Zauberwort" (II, 377).
Also: "Definition ist ein Faktum. Die Bezeichnung dieses Faktums
ist die gemeinhin sogenannte Definition" (II, 383). These fragments
show that at the back of Novalis' mind there are Aristotle's "Realdefinitionen (Angaben des Wesens, Begriffskonstruktionen) und
Nominaldefinitionen (Benennungen)" (these formulations are found
in W. Dubislav, *Die Definition*, 3rd ed., Leipzig, 1931, p. 7). Novalis
emphasizes the realness of definition. As soon as a definition, no
matter how arbitrary, is made, it becomes a fact. By definition we
create and generate things and ideas. Novalis' conception of
definition as a genetic notion parallels the concept of "schöpferische
Definition" in formal discussions of definition (see Dubislav, p. 59).
Such a definition is like a magic word: if you want something, you
define it, and it comes into existence. Novalis' magic idealism rests
largely on this idea of creative, or genetic definition. The necessity
for anticipation of the basic structure of a system, when making
definitions to introduce the system, is stressed by Novalis in the

following fragment: "Einfache Definitionen gibts nicht zuerst – je mehr man zugleich definiert – desto richtiger wird jede einzelne Definition. Definieren en masse – Wissenschaft. Die Definition ist die Konstruktionsformel der Begriffe etc." (III, 161). The more definitions are made simultaneously, the better the chance is that they will be consistent. Somehow definition must be reduced to a universal principle. Novalis weighs the possibility that God is the source of all definitions: "Definition und Klassifikation der Wissenschaften – notwendiges und vollständiges Prinzip der Definition und der davon abhängenden besonderen Definitionen und Klassifikationen. Das höchste Prinzip ist der höchste Grad. Dem höchsten realen Grad entspricht der höchste ideale Grad. Sollte Gott das Ideal des Grades, und die Definition von Gott – der Keim aller Definitionen sein? Sollte die Definition Gottes und die Definition des Infinitesimalgrades unendlich sein, so müssen wir bei der Definition eines Mittelgrades id est eines endlichen Grades anfangen – oder mit der allgemeinen Definition des Grades überhaupt" (III, 207).

Axiom. Another crucial mathematical concept discussed by Novalis is axiom, or postulate. His preoccupation with this concept is also rooted in his time, during which the time-honored puzzle about one of Euclid's axioms began to resolve itself. Although Euclid's *Elements* had been accepted as valid for about two thousand years, there is one point in it that was challenged from the earliest times, namely, his parallelity axiom: "If a straight line falling on two other straight lines makes the interior angles on the same side of the line less than two right angles, the two straight lines, if produced indefinitely, meet on that side on which the angles are less than two right angles" (as quoted in L. R. Eisenhart, *Coordinate Geometry*, Boston, etc., 1939, p. 280). Since this axiom did not appear to be simple enough to be self-evident, attempts were made to convert it into a theorem by deducing it from the other axioms. In 1733 Saccheri tried to furnish the proof by a reduction to the absurd. He replaced the parallel axiom by an axiom contradicting it, in the hope of producing inconsistent conclusions. Instead of obtaining the contradictions, he laid the foundation for non-Euclidean geometry. This branch was formally proposed by Lobachevsky and Bolyai around 1825 and proved in its consistency by Cayley in 1859. Novalis sensed the uneasiness about the foundations of mathematics in his time and was induced to probe into the meaning of axiom.

In the preceding chapter we already quoted Novalis' following translated excerpt from Hemsterhuis' *Aristée*: "Axiomen beruhn auf sinnlicher Überzeugung. Die künstliche, gemachte Überzeugung geht vom Axiom aus. Die letztere hat die erstere verdrängt – Sie ist so scharf umrissen – jene hingegen so einfach als möglich – daher aber so unscheinbar – Sie ist auch mitteilbar, welches jene nicht ist" (II, 293). Novalis says with Hemsterhuis that axioms are based on "sensuous conviction." He is referring to geometrical axioms which originally were regarded as propositions obvious to the senses, in this case, to the sense of vision, whereas in modern mathematics all such considerations are regarded as irrelevant and superfluous. In Novalis' time, axioms were regarded as unprovable propositions, the "truth" of which should be obvious to any person endowed with a normal and healthy dose of "common sense." In modern, formalistic treatment of mathematics, axioms are regarded as unprovable, or rather unproved, propositions with the only restriction that a given set of axioms shall not give rise to contradictory results. The modern mathematician does not rely on sense perception, or on some vague notion of obviousness, or of common sense. Novalis observes, in the passage just quoted, that once an axiom has been accepted, it generates artificial, make-believe conviction ("künstliche, gemachte Überzeugung"), *i.e.*, more complicated results are not immediately, if they are at all, obvious to the senses. This is an important insight on the part of Novalis at a time prior to publication of non-Euclidean considerations. Then Novalis proceeds to state: "Die letztere hat die erstere verdrängt," *i.e.*, the feigned or simulated conviction has superseded the sensuous conviction. Novalis is thus aware of the gradual supersession of the empirical basis of mathematics by the postulational foundation. One of ancient axioms of geometry which states that there is one and only one line passing through any two distinct points was obvious to the sense of vision and therefore assumed the status of truth. Nowadays, axioms are simply assumed to be true, or just stated without reference to truth or falsity. However, as soon as propositions are made in terms of these axioms, the propositions may be regarded as true or false with respect to the axioms, or as deducible or not deducible from the axioms, or as consistent or inconsistent with the set of axioms. In the following excerpt from Dumas the emphasis is on the old conception of "absolute truth:" "Vollkommene Überzeugung ist das Gefühl von absoluter Wahrheit. Absolute Wahrheit für uns ist Identität der Anschauung und des Wesens eines Objekts. Jedes echte Axiom ist der Ausdruck eines solchen absolut Wahren" (II, 285). Two final comments of Novalis on the postulation of axioms will attest to Novalis' conception of axiom as independent of physical reality: "Voraussetzen bedeutet, vom Gegenstande gebraucht, eine Handlung vor der Existenz, eine Antizipation – denn das Setzende wird erst möglich durch ein Setzen – dieses Setzen ist aber ursprünglich gleich – gegensetzen" (II, 132). "Axiome und Postulate bezeichnen das theoretische (a) und praktische (b) Wissensvermögen überhaupt. Aufgaben bezeichnen den Trieb. Auflösung und Beweis das analytische (ad a) und synthetische (ad b) Vermögen" (II, 256).

Theorem. Novalis distinguishes between what theorems are and what they should be. Like Leibniz, d'Alembert, and Goethe, he finds that most theorems are tautological, *i.e.*, the conclusion of a theorem is merely a more succinct restatement of its hypothesis: "Die meisten mathematischen Sätze gleichen alle dem Satz a = a. Jeder mathematische Satz ist eine Gleichung" (III, 21). However, in accordance with Kant's conception of a theorem as a synthetic, and not analytic, judgment, Novalis demands: "Lehrsätze müssen etwas Neues aussagen, etwas was nicht in der Definition (Bezeichnung der eigentümlichen Natur) begriffen ist. Sie müssen, nach der Kunstsprache, synthetisch sein" (III, 20).

The specific theorems marginally annotated by Novalis are the binomial (III, 37, 79, 201) and Pythagorean (III, 22) theorems.

Proof. We have discussed Novalis' fragments on definition, axiom, and theorem. The concept linking and separating the three is proof, since theorems are proved in terms of definitions, axioms, and possibly other theorems. Novalis observes: "Der Beweis ist eine indirekte Konstruktion – ein mathematisches Experiment – ein Rezept" (III, 21). Also: "Grundproblem der Mathematik. (Gibt es ein mathematisches (Leben) Genie? Wie ist es möglich? Erstere Auflösung liefert den Satz – die andere den Beweis, die Konstruktionsmethode dazu)" (III, 25) (cf. also Chapter II, Section 3). Proof is an indirect construction of a theorem from definitions and axioms. Proof, furthermore, is a "mathematical experiment," *i.e.*, obtained by experimentation with definitions and axioms. Proof is a "recipe," Novalis says, using his favorite medical metaphor. A recipe is a prescription, and proof, likewise, is a prescription of the steps leading to the establishment of a theorem. In order to extend the mathematical method of demonstration to a more general range, Novalis postulates an isomorphism between calculating and thinking: "Der Beweis ist die Rechnung, deren Resultat der zu beweisende Satz ist. Rechnen und Denken ist eins..." (III, 24). However, as soon as this extension has taken place and the solid ground of mathematics has been abandoned, proof loses its attribute of absolute certainty, and on this state Novalis remarks in a Kantian vein: "Alles ist demonstrabel = alles ist antinomisch. Es gibt eine Sphäre, wo jeder Beweis ein Zirkel – oder ein Irrtum – wo nichts demonstrabel ist – dies ist die Sphäre der gebildeten goldenen Zeit" (III, 227). No sooner Novalis seems to attain for himself clarification of the nature of proof, when he already begins to cast doubt on its validity. He is reminded of the antinomy of pure reason, as presented by Kant in the *Kritik der reinen Vernunft*, where first a thesis is proved, then the corresponding antithesis (*e.g.*, the world has a beginning in time; the world has no beginning). Novalis is also reminded of the constant danger of getting entangled in a circular proof. He hopes that in some Utopia all proving will be superfluous, and hence circular, or circular, and hence superfluous. Perhaps a generalization of proof along the lines of Fichte's Science of Knowledge ("Wissenschaftslehre") would yield a science of knowledge of mathematics: "Versuch, das zu beweisen und aufzulösen – zu konstruieren, was die Mathematik nicht beweist oder auflöst – Wissenschaftslehre der Mathematik. Applikatur der Aufgaben und Lehrsätze – Verknüpfung derselben – Scientifizierung der Mathematik" (III, 257).

2. GEOMETRY

General Remarks. Novalis defines: "Die Mathematik der Kräfte ist die Mechanik. Die Mathematik der Gestalten ist die Geometrie" (III, 17). ,,Kräfte" is here not only used as "force" in the usual physical sense, but also as a potential, a function, something that is effective but intangible, an entity not unlike the monad of Leibniz. Mechanics is the mathematics of such forces, geometry is the mathematics of shapes and figures. Mechanics is dynamic, geometry is static. Mechanics deals with inward elusive forces; geometry, with outward, visible characteristics. As the embodiments of the static and dynamic, geometry and mechanics become spiritual forces to Novalis. These forces are effective beyond their respective proper domains, as exemplified by the influence on philosophy and science of the atomistic and dynamic views of matter and energy and the various attempts to fuse them: "Die Verwandschaft der Geometrie und Mechanik mit den höchsten Problemen des menschlichen Geistes überhaupt leuchtet aus dem atomistischen und dynamischen Sektenstreit hervor" (III, 229).

To clarify further the distinction between geometry and mechanics, Novalis identifies geometry with "Plastik," mechanics with "Akustik." "Geometrie ist transzendentale Zeichenkunst – Plastik. (Mechanik – transzendentale Akustik etc.)" (III, 160), or, "Geometrie und Mechanik verhalten sich wie Plastik und Musik" (III, 118). Thus geometry is also opposed to arithmetic, because Novalis links music with arithmetic (see Chapter IV, Section 7). Since geometry is related to "den höchsten Problemen des menschlichen Geistes überhaupt," it should perhaps be treated in the most general theory of external characteristics: "Sollte die Geometrie zum Teil nach der Lehre von den äusseren Kennzeichen überhaupt behandelt werden können?" (III, 31). What does Novalis mean by a general theory of external characteristics? An explanation of such a theory is suggested by certain developments in scientific methods of classification in the eighteenth century. The Linnaean system of classifying plants by their external characteristics had turned a seemingly chaotic agglomeration of plants into a vegetable kingdom ruled by law and order. Part of the classification was based on the number and geometric patterns of stamens and pistils. This method became definitive after the 1758 edition of the *Systema naturae* (1735) by Linnaeus, the well-known botanist of the time. Werner, Novalis' teacher, and the most authoritative geologist of the time, had raised mineralogy to the status of a science through his method of classifying minerals by external characteristics, and, in this connection, Novalis speaks of the "Mathematizität der oryktognostischen Klassifikation" (III, 228). In exploring the mathematicity of Werner's classification, Novalis also weighed the possibility of determining the algebraic pattern of the theory of external characteristics. For this reason he wonders in the following fragment: "Sollte die Geometrie *zum Teil* nach der Lehre von den äusseren Kennzeichen überhaupt behandelt werden?" (III, 31). Then he states more positively: "Allgemeine Oryktognosie – oder algebraische Oryktognosie. Grundsätze der Lehre von den äusseren Kennzeichen überhaupt" (III, 30). As a final explanatory note on Novalis' preoccupation with a possible mathematical general theory of external characteristics we may again refer to Leibniz' search for a "characteristica generalis," which had led him to the mathematical theory of permutations and combinations.

Geometry may, in the opinion of Novalis, begin either with real bodies, or with imaginary points: "Anfang der Geometrie mit wirklichen Körpern – Anfang mit Punkten. Figurensystem. – Raumbegrenzungs- und Raumerfüllungssystem" (III, 151). Elementary geometry is higher than higher geometry, because the highest and purest is also the simplest. The more complicated and involved a science becomes, the more readily it loses its purity, Novalis holds. "Das Höchste und Reinste ist das Gemeinste, das Verständlichste. Daher ist auch die Elementargeometrie höher als die höhere Geometrie. Je schwieriger und verwickelter eine Wissenschaft wird, desto abgeleiteter, unreiner und vermischter ist sie" (III, 20). On this point Novalis is in agreement with Goethe.

Point. Ever since Euclid had defined a point, philosophers have been endeavoring to define and interpret this concept in various contexts. Novalis adds his own comments to this discussion: "Der Punkt kann nicht als bewegt gedacht werden" (II, 192). "Philosophie des Punkts – Seine Entstehung" (III, 151). Euclid's definition of a point as that which has no part had been repeated for two thousand years, until Hilbert eliminated this definition as useless for strict mathematical argumentation. Hilbert introduces point, along with straight lines and planes, as undefined elements: "Wir denken drei verschiedene Systeme von Dingen: die Dinge des ersten Systems nennen wir *Punkte* und bezeichnen sie mit $A, B, C, \ldots$; die Dinge des zweiten Systems nennen wir *Geraden* und bezeichnen sie mit, $a, b, c, \ldots$; die Dinge des dritten Systems nennen wir *Ebenen* und bezeichnen sie mit α, β, γ; die Punkte heissen auch die *Elemente der linearen Geometrie*, die Punkte und Geraden heissen *Elemente der ebenen Geometrie*, und die Punkte, Geraden und Ebenen heissen die *Elemente der räumlichen Geometrie* oder *des Raums*" (David Hilbert, *Grundlagen der Geometrie*, 7th ed., Leipzig und Berlin, 1930, p. 2). Points, lines, and planes are not defined, or are by definition undefined, because an explicit definition of these elements is not required for the system. However, propositions made in terms of these elements, restrict their meaning and post-define them, as it were. Thus we are again reminded of Novalis exploration of the relative priority of definitions and the system resting on them.

Line. The definition of a straight line has undergone a change similar to that of a point. Euclid defined it as length without breadth, which, again, is a definition useless from the mathematical point of view. Hilbert introduces it as an undefined element, as we have just seen. Novalis juxtaposes straight lines with curves (krumme Linien). To him straight lines symbolize the schematism and regularity of man's mind, whereas curves represent unpredictable nature and organic life: "Krumme Linie – Sieg der freien Natur über die Regel" (III, 101). "Alle krummen Linien entstehen nur durch sich selbst, wie Leben nur durch Leben entsteht" (III, 151).

Circle. Novalis states: "Simplizität des Zirkels – seine leichte Konstruktion. Übergänge der Kegelschnitte ineinander. Entstehung aus Gleichungen gerader, entgegengesetzter Linien" (III, 151). "Auch instinktartig ist der Zirkel der Figuren Kanon" (III, 251). To Novalis the circle is the canonical form of all geometric figures, including the conical sections. However, at the bottom of the ancient problem of squaring the circle is the supposition that the square must be regarded as the protoform of all figures: "Anwendung der vorigen Bemerkung auf die Quadratur des Zirkels. Ihr liegt die Hypothese oder das Postulat zum Grunde, dass der Urtyp der Zirkelform das Quadrat sei. Das Problem des Zirkels ist also das Problem der Reduktion aller Figuren aufs Quadrat – oder umgekehrt aller Figuren auf die Runde. Je grösser wir die Teilungszahl dieser Figur machen – eine desto genauere Auflösung erhalten wir. Eine unendliche Teilungszahl gibt uns eine unendlich

genaue Auflösung. Differential- und Integralrechnung" (III, 177).
The problem of squaring the circle with straightedge and compass was proved to be insoluble by Lindemann in 1882. But for over two millenia prior to this date, philosophers, mathematicians, and laymen racked their brains in an attempt to solve the problem. The problem of squaring the circle was first posed, along with two others: doubling the cube and trisecting an angle under the same restrictions, by Greek mathematicians. Merriman indicates the historical context of these problems as follows: "Joined by its sister problems, that of trisecting an arbitrary angle and that of constructing a square equal in area to that of a given circle, the problem of duplicating a cube was food for centuries of thought, of experiment, of frustration, of mystery – and of fruitfulness" (Gaylord M. Merriman, *To Discover Mathematics*, New York, 1942, p. 125). These problems came to be regarded as transcending the boundaries of human intelligence and hence were classified in the same category as the problems of finding the philosopher's stone or the elixir of life. For this reason, Novalis equates the question "Lässt sich ein Zirkel quadrieren?" with the fundamental question of Kant's *Kritik der reinen Vernunft*: "Sind synthetische Urteile a priori möglich?" (cf. III, 230-231; see also Chapter II, Section 3).

Thus Novalis' fragments on geometry in general, and on the concept of circle in particular, reveal associations with mystical thought. Dietrich Mahnke and Maurice Besset take Novalis' cryptic note "mystische Geometrie" (III, 248) as a clue for their interpretation of some of Novalis' fragments on geometry in mystical contexts.

3. ARITHMETIC AND ALGEBRA

General Comments. Novalis seldom discusses details of arithmetic proper, but is usually concerned with this branch of mathematics in the extended sense of "arithmetica universalis." For example: "Unsere Buchstaben sollen Zahlen, unsere Sprache Arithmetik werden" (III, 18). "Philosophische Arithmetik – reine – höhere – spezielle und angewandte Arithmetik" (III, 132). Similarly, algebra is generalized: "Die Basis aller Wissenschaften und Künste muss eine Wissenschaft und Kunst sein – die man der Algebra vergleichen kann" (III, 76). Novalis advocates, or considers the possibility of, applying algebra to metaphysics (II, 188, 280), music (III, 127, 206), and poetry (III, 118). Algebra includes the theory of general relations: "Die Lehre von den Verhältnissen gehört in die Algebra" (III, 241). Hence algebra is not confined to number only. In fact, pure algebra does not deal with number at all: "In der reinen Algeber kommen keine Zahlen vor" (III, 23). Novalis thought of his universal mathematics as a system that would, through progressive generalizations, include all knowledge and all spheres of mental, volitional, emotional, and aesthetic existence. One such stage of generalization had been achieved by the expansion of arithmetic into algebra, by the replacement of the distinct number by the unspecified algebraic letter. The next stage would be the transition from quantitative to qualitative relationships. In Section 3 of the preceding chapter we already discussed Novalis' preoccupation with "Übersetzung der Qualität in Quantität und umgekehrt" (III, 248) and "relative Mathematik" (III, 22) in preparation of an extension of mathematics from Kant's mathematical categories of quantity and quality to the dynamical categories of relation and modality. Thus, in delimiting the range of mathematics, Novalis had gone beyond Kant, whereas Kant had gone beyond the leading mathematicians of his day by his designation of both quantity and quality as mathematical categories. Whereas Kant had extended mathematics beyond the category of quantity, and Novalis had said "Reine Mathematik hat nichts mit Grösse zu tun" (III, 325), the noted eighteenth-century mathematician Euler still confined mathematics to the realm of magnitude: "...indem die Mathematik überhaupt nichts anderes ist als eine Wissenschaft der Grössen, und welche Mittel ausfindig macht, wie man dieselben ausmessen soll," although Euler's own work transcends this range (see *Vollständige Anleitung zur Algebra*, Leonardi Eulera *Opera Omnia*, Series prima, Volumen primum, Lipsiae et Berolini, 1910, p. 9; first published in St. Petersburg in 1770). Modern mathematicians disagree with such a narrow definition of mathematics. Some branches of mathematics deal mainly with quality, not quantity. For example, B. v. Kerékjártó defines topology, a branch of mathematics, as follows: "Die *Topologie* oder *Analysis Situs* ist derjenige Teil der Geometrie, der die bei stetigen Transformationen ungeändert bleibenden Eigenschaften der Gebilde untersucht. Diese sind Zusammenhangs- und Lagenverhältnisse, sozusagen Eigenschaften von qualitativer Natur" (*Vorlesungen über Topologie*, Die Grundlehren der mathematischen Wissenschaften, ed. R. Courant et al., VIII, Berlin, 1923, p. 1).

In the light of these progressive generalizations of "arithmetica universalis" from numbers and figures through letters toward the most inclusive system of concepts we can read intelligently the following verses of Novalis:

> *Wenn nicht mehr Zahlen und Figuren*
> *Sind Schlüssel aller Kreaturen,*
> *Wenn die so singen, oder küssen*
> *Mehr als die Tiefgelehrten wissen,*

Wenn sich die Welt ins freie Leben,
Und in die Welt wird zurückbegeben,
Wenn dann sich wieder Licht und Schatten
Zu echter Klarheit werden gatten,
Und man in Märchen und Gedichten
Erkennt die ewgen Weltgeschichten,
Dann fliegt vor einem geheimen Wort
Das ganze verkehrte Wesen fort.

These lines are found among the paralipomena to "Heinrich von Ofterdingen" (I, 244, 251). The continuation of this fragmentary novel was to include a sublimation of the sciences, including mathematics. This intent is indicated by several of the paralipomena to the novel: "Allerhand Wissenschaften poetisiert, auch die Mathematik im Wettstreit," "Klingsohr – Poesie der Wissenschaften" (I, 242). According to Tieck's report on the continuation of "Ofterdingen," Novalis intended to devote one of the six sequels to this novel to physics, *i.e.*, to the physical sciences, which presumably includes mathematics: "Es war die Absicht des Dichters, nach Vollendung des "Ofterdingen" noch sechs Romane zu schreiben, in denen er seine Ansichten der Physik, des bürgerlichen Lebens, der Handlung, der Geschichte, der Politik und der Liebe, so wie im "Ofterdingen" der Poesie niederlegen wollte" (I, 250).

Novalis sometimes speaks of "kritische Algeber" (III, 206): "Algeber und kombinatorische Analysis sind durchaus kritisch. Die unbekannten Glieder findet man durch Syllogistik – kombinatorische Operationen der gegebenen Glieder. (*Vide* Kants Verfahren)" (III, 229). In his *Kritik der reinen Vernunft* Kant had set the critical approach to problems of pure reason above dogmaticism and scepticism. In accordance with this method, Novalis, in his turn, sifts, weighs, and combines his ideas critically, avoiding dogmaticism and scepticism, *i.e.*, the convenient, uncritical acceptance of an idea on the one hand, and the equally convenient categorical denial of an idea on the other hand. The general algebra that Novalis hoped to attain should also be critical. Pure algebra and pure philosophy would merge into a universal science:"Allgemeine Sätze sind nichts als algebraische Formeln. Die reine Philosophie ist daher gerade so etwas wie die Letternalgebra. So eine Formel kann ein Gattungs-, ein Klassen- und Lokalzeichen sein" (II, 383).

Novalis also expresses his views on the demarcation of the boundaries between algebra and other branches of mathematics. He is particularly concerned with a distinction between algebra and analysis. We find among his fragments a brief note specifying "Unterschied der Analysis und Algebra" (II, 333) as well as more specific comments: "Die Differentialrechnung ist die Kritik – die Integralrechnung – die Auflösung – jene lehrt die Daten ordnen – zu Gleichungen – diese die Gleichungen auflösen. Jene ist die Algeber – diese die Analysis – denn Algeber und Analysis verhalten sich auch so zueinander" (III, 236). However, more generally, algebra and analysis are one science: "Sie, die Algeber und die sogenannte Analysis machen eine Wissenschaft aus" (III, 99).

The distinction between analysis and algebra was of some concern to the combinatorial school. Klügel writes in his essay in Hindenburg's collection *Der polynomische Lehrsatz*, p. 48: "Die Analysis endlicher Grössen besteht aus zwei Hauptteilen, die zwar durch gegenseitige Hilfsleistungen mit einander verbunden sind, aber nicht einer auf dem anderen beruhen... Diese beiden Teile sind die Algebra und die Analysis im engeren Verstande. Jene beschäftigt sich mit den Eigenschaften der Gleichungen, der Zusammensetzung und Entwicklung derselben... Die eigentliche Analysis hat zum Gegenstand überhaupt die Formen der Grössen, nämlich teils die Umwandlung einer Form in eine andere, teils die Darstellung der Glieder einer stetigen Fortschreitung durch die zugeordneten Glieder einer anderen Reihe nach irgend einem Gesetze..." Novalis' discussion of the boundaries between algebra and analysis are no doubt at least in part induced by the preoccupation of the combinatorial school with this problem.

Number. Novalis probes into the origin of this concept. He believes that the basic function of human reason underlying the origin of the concept of number is counting: "Wer zuerst bis zwei zu zählen verstand, sah, wenn ihm auch selbst das Fortzählen noch schwer ward, doch die Möglichkeit einer unendlichen Fortzählung nach denselben Gesetzen" (III, 347). Novalis' association of the origin of number with the mental process of enumeration parallels both the conception of the origin of number of some modern philosophers and historians of mathematics and the modern postulational definition of number as part of a sequence with a given definition of the relation of one of its elements to its predecessor. In contemplating the origin of number, Novalis probes further into its mysterious aspects: "Merkwürdige, geheimnisvolle Zahlen. Wie das Zählen noch neu war, so mussten oft vorkommende Zahlen beim Zählen wirklicher Dinge – charakteristische bleibende Zahlen wie z. B. die 10 Finger etc. – und andere frappante Zahlenphänomene die Einbildungskraft der Menschen aufs lebhafteste beschäftigen und sie in der Wissenschaft der Zahlen einen tiefverborgenen Schatz von Weisheit – einen Schlüssel zu allen verschlossenen Türen der Natur ahnden lassen" (III, 151). Novalis sometimes touches on the ontological aspect of number: "Der

Begriff des Zählens bezieht sich nur auf das einfache Sein – es ist ein einfaches Fixieren dieses einfachen Zustandes" (II, 206). Counting may be homogeneous or heterogeneous: "Über das homogene und heterogene Zählen – Zählen des Gleichartigen – Zählen des Ungleichartigen – Eins durch das andere "(III, 159). Numbers are abstracted in counting and are therefore, not unlike poetry, freely created: "Alles aus nichts erschaffene Reale, wie z. B. die Zahlen und die abstrakten Ausdrücke – hat eine wunderbare Verwandtschaft mit Dingen einer anderen Welt, mit unendlichen Reihen sonderbarer Kombinationen und Verhältnisse, gleichsam mit einer (mathematischen und abstrakten Welt an sich, mit einer) poetischen, mathematischen und abstrakten Welt" (III, 167f.).

Like Goethe, Novalis regards both numbers, the mathematical elements, and words, the literary elements, as strata of an all-inclusive symbolic language: "Die allgemeinen Ausdrücke der scholastischen Philosophie haben sehr viel Ähnlichkeit mit den Zahlen – daher ihr mystischer Gebrauch – ihre Personifikation – ihr musikalischer Genuss – ihre unendliche Kombination" (III, 167). Words and numbers are often discussed by Novalis under the same categories: "Zahlen und Wort Gestaltenlehre z. B. Reihen etc. Zahlen und Wort Mechanik – Geschwindigkeitslehre.)" (III, 172). "Zahlen sind wie Worte, Erscheinungen, Repräsentationen kat' exochen. Ihre Verhältnisse sind Weltverhältnisse" (III, 295). "Zahlen und Worte sind Zeitdimensionsfiguren und Zeichen. Wort- und Zahlfigurationen" (III, 260) (See also Chapter IV, Section "Mathematics and Language").

Magnitude. Novalis' discussion of "Grösse" (quantity, magnitude, or entity) is found mainly in the section entitled "Mathematische Fragmente" (III, 20-23). We cite one of his general formulations of the concept: "Der Begriff Grösse drückt das Verhältnis zu einem gemeinschaftlichen Begriff, oder Ganzem, zu einer Einheit wenn man will, aus. Der Anteil am gemeinschaftlichen Begriff bestimmt die Grösse – Dieser gemeinschaftliche Begriff mag nun Zahl oder Kraft, oder Ausdehnung, oder Richtung, oder Stoff, oder Lage – oder Helligkeit oder sonst des etwas sein" (III, 21). Now according to Novalis, the task of mathematics is to determine the dissimilarities in similarities with reference to a common characteristic. But mathematics also determines the similarities in the peculiar characteristics: "Die Mathematik bestimmt den Unterschied im Gemeinschaftlichen – die Ungleichheiten im Gleichen. Sie unterscheidet in Beziehung auf das gemeinschaftliche Merkmal. Und die Mathematik bestimmt auch (setzt) die Ähnlichkeiten, die Gemeinheiten im eigentümlichen Merkmal. Dort macht sie Unterschiede – hier hebt sie Unterschiede auf" (III, 22). Thus mathematics deals with various magnitudes and entities transcending the more restricted range of purely quantitative units. He also deals with quantitative magnitude. He points out that a quantity may be expressed or approximated by a series. For example, 3 is represented by the series

$$"2 + \tfrac{1}{2} + \tfrac{1}{4} + \tfrac{1}{8} + \text{etc.}" \qquad (\text{III, 23})$$

He specifies: "Ist die Reihe geschlossen, bestimmt, so ist auch die Grösse bestimmt – ist die Reihe unendlich, so ists auch die Grösse" (III, 23). "Infinite" here refers to the limit approached by the terms of the series, and not only to the number of terms, which is usually infinite anyhow, since an infinite series may approach a finite limit, as is exemplified by Novalis' above-quoted own example of a convergent series. By a series that is "geschlossen und bestimmt" Novalis means a convergent series, by an infinite series, *i.e.*, a series with an "infinite limit," a divergent series. The meaning of his fragment is, therefore, equivalent to saying that a quantity is finite or infinite according to the convergence or divergence, respectively, of the series representing the quantity.

Novalis further denies the existence of absolute, indivisible, nondecomposable magnitudes. A magnitude is either divisible into its component parts, or may be approximated by a series, or in some other way: "Jede Grösse ist ein Aggregat – ein Teilbares, eine Reihe, Kette – eine schlechthin einfache Grösse gibt es nicht" (III, 23). A magnitude is best comprehended with regard to its opposite, or as an unknown in terms of known magnitudes: "Ich verstehe eine Grösse, wenn ich in ihrer Äquation auf der anderen Seite eine Funktion der Gegengrösse habe. Eine Hauptantithese der Mathematik ist, **bekannte und unbekannte Grössen**" (III, 79).

Novalis' observations on the concept of "Grösse" again indicate his preoccupation with an extension of mathematics beyond its usual domain. On the one hand, mathematics is to be extended beyond the mere manipulation of quantitative magnitudes of entities. On the other hand, or rather, from the other end, this extension is to be effected by an expansion of the concept of "Grösse" itself. Thus he can state ideally: "Reine Mathematik hat nichts mit Grösse zu tun" (III, 325).

Basic Operations. Novalis examines the interrelations of various basic operations: "Die Verhältnisse der drei Rechnungsarten 1. + und − 2. × und : 3. a^n und $\sqrt{}$ versteh ich recht gut; wie verhält sich aber das Differentiieren und Integrieren und das Verwandeln in Reihen und Reduzieren der Reihen dazu? Das Logarithmisieren ist ein Appendix zu Nr. 3. Die Bruchlogarithmen sind, wie die Bruchexponenten, nur Approximationen zu Rationallogarithmen und Exponenten" (III, 21). Novalis points to the elementary facts of arithmetic and algebra that subtraction is the inverse of addition, multiplication an abbreviation of repeated addition, division the inverse of multiplication, etc. However, he is uncertain about the classification of differentiation and integration within the same framework of distinctions, *i.e.*, in terms of the other basic operations. A modern mathematician may feel that the very attempt to classify differentiation and integration in the same category as the traditionally basic arithmetical and algebraic operations is questionable from the outset. To meet such a possible objection we must again consider the state of mathematics toward the end of the eighteenth century. We could cite, in particular, Lagrange's *Théorie des fonctions analytiques*, where he attempted to reduce differential calculus to algebra by offering a purely algebraic process of finding the derivative (See Chapter II, Section 4). Lagrange's book was published in 1797. The German translation of this work, of which Novalis owned a copy, came out in 1798, and the fragment by Novalis inquiring about the classification of differentiation and integration in terms of algebraic or arithmetic operations was written during 1798-1799, according to the Havenstein-Kluckhohn chronology of Novalis' fragments. It is manifest that in the contexts of the history of mathematics Novalis' question was very timely. Moreover, Novalis' cautious formulation of the problem as a question proved prudent, because Lagrange's opinions on this matter, though highly authoritative, were soon discarded.

Some of Novalis' fragments deal with mathematical operations with a view to their extension to more general philosophical problems: "Synthetische Kalküle z. B. Addieren und Subtrahieren – Addieren und Multiplizieren – etc.... Erschöpfen der Arten des Kalkül durch kombinatorische Kunst. Um das ordentlich zu bewerkstelligen, muss man aber erst die Begriffe der einzelnen Kalküle kritisch betrachtet haben. – Der gewöhnliche arithmetische Kalkül im ganzen ist ein kombinatorisches Addieren etc." (III, 25). Mathematical operations reveal the art of defining and combining definitions. The theory of numbers is a preparatory stage in the development of a philosophical calculus: "Kalkül = Kunst, Bestimmungen zu verbinden, oder Kunst zu bestimmen überhaupt, z. B. aus gegebenen Bestimmungen nicht gegebene Bestimmungen zu finden. Rechnungslehre – Bestimmungsverwandtschaftslehre. Die Zahlenlehre macht die Rechnungslehre möglich – bereitet sie vor" (III, 153). Novalis contends that some day a calculus of philosophical abstraction will enable man to analyze satisfactorily empirical data. One is reminded of the extraordinary ascendency of statistical method since Novalis' death. However, Novalis meant more than statistical analysis of data: "Man geht mit den Erfahrungen und Experimenten noch viel zu sorglos um – Man versteht sie nicht zu benutzen – Man betrachtet zu wenig die Erfahrungen – als Data zur Auflösung und mannigfaltigen Kombination zum Kalkül – ... Der Abstraktionskalkül der Philosophie ist vollkommen dem Infinitesimalkalkül zu vergleichen" (III, 156). Another fragment stresses the philosophical aspects of mathematical operations: "*Mathematik.* Allgemeiner Begriff der Multiplikation – nicht bloss der mathematischen – so der Division, Addition etc. Vorzüglich interessant ist diese philosophische Betrachtung der bisher bloss mathematischen Begriffe und Operationen – bei den Potenzen, Wurzeln, Differentialen, Integralen, Reihen – Kurven – und Direkten – Funktionen" (III, 79). In Chapter IV, Section "Mathematics and Philosophy," more analogies between mathematical and philosophical operations will be discussed.

4. ANALYSIS

General Comments. Novalis' general discussion of the meaning and the origin of "Analyse" and "Analysis" is not restricted to mathematical analysis. Analysis is diametrically opposed to synthesis, yet both are inseparably linked: "Der analytische Gang muss ein synthetischer sein et vice versa – es kommt nur darauf an, an welches Ende man sich stellt. Der analytische ist durch eine Synthese, der synthetische durch eine Analyse bedingt" (II' 74). Synthesis is subjective, analysis is objective and formal: "Synthetisches Verfahren ist nach der Weise des reinen Ich – analytisches Verfahren nach der Weise der blossen Form" (II, 240). These opposites are reconciled in God: "Gott ist die Sphäre aller Analyse und Synthese – ein theoretisch und praktisch notwendiger Begriff" (II, 268). Since synthesis is subjective and analysis is objective, pure science proceeds from analysis to synthesis: "Die reine Wissenschaft geht analytisch id est sie geht mittelst der Analyse auf Synthese" (II, 270). Reflections on analysis led Novalis to a consideration of combinatorial analysis, one of his favorate subjects. Combinatorial analysis must be exhaustive: "In der Kombinationslehre liegt das Prinzip der Vollständigkeit – so wie in der Analysis – oder der Kunst, aus gegebenen Datis die unbekannten Glieder zu finden" (III, 209). The danger involved in striving for exhaustive thinking is getting entangled in a labyrinth of erratic speculation. The danger is diminished by the pursuit of a definite goal that unifies and directs our thought: "Die blosse Analyse – die blosse Experimentation und Beobachtung führt in unabsehliche Räume und schlechthin in die Unendlichkeit. – Ist sie poetischer Natur und Absicht, so mags sein; sonst muss man absolut einen Zweck – mit Recht einer genannt – haben oder setzen, damit man sich nicht in diese Spekulation, wie in ein Labyrinth – einem Wahnwitzigen völlig gleich, verliert. Hier ist der Sitz der so berüchtigten Spekulation – des verschrienen, falschen Mystizism – des Glaubens an die Ergründung der Dinge an sich" (III, 169). The poetical analyst may be permitted to drift to infinity, but the ideal analyst must subject his divinatory powers to strict rules: "Die Analysis ist (die Divinations- oder) die Erfindungskunst auf Regeln gebracht -- ihre mögliche Ausbreitung und Vervollkommnung" (III, 162).

We shall now consider Novalis' meditations on analysis in the more restricted sense of mathematical analysis, in particular, infinitesimal calculus.

Infinitesimal Calculus. Novalis compares the methods of Newton and Leibniz, the two inventors of calculus, and points to the difficulties underlying the foundations of their methods: "Die Verschiedenheit der Leibnizischen und Newtonschen Vorstellungsart von der Rechnung des Unendlichen beruht auf demselben Grunde als die Verschiedenheit der atomistischen und Vibrations- oder ätherischen Theorie. Die Fluxion und das Differential sind die entgegengesetzten Anschauungen des mathematischen Elements – beide zusammen machen die mathematische Substanz aus. Es beruht auf dem Satze $x + y = +$. Dieses Plus ist das Differential oder die Fluxion der Funktionen von x und y. Die proportionelle Einteilung dieses Plus ist die Hauptschwierigkeit dieses Kalküls. Leibniz nennt den Infinitesimalkalkül auch die Analysis Indivisibilium (Steter Grössen – stetig übergehender Grössen). Infinitesimalkalkül heisst eigentlich Rechnung, Einteilung oder Messung des Nichteingeteilten – Nichtvergleichbaren – Unermesslichen" (III, 229). The main difficulty in the foundation of calculus is, according to Novalis, the "proportional division of the plus," *i.e.*, of the differential. In order to explain what he means by this, we consider Newton's definition of "fluxion" as contained in his treatise *Quadrature of Curves* (1704): "In the same time that x, by flowing, becomes $x + 0$, the power x^n becomes $(x + 0)^n$, i.e., by the method of infinite series

$$. \qquad x^n + n0 \times {}^{n-1} + \frac{n^2 - n}{2} 0^2 x^{n-2} + \text{etc.}$$

and the increments

$$. \qquad 0 \quad \text{and} \quad n0 \times {}^{n-1} + \frac{n^2 - n}{2} 0^2 \times {}^{n-2} + \text{etc.}$$

are to one another as

$$. \qquad 1 \quad \text{to} \quad nx^{n-1} + \frac{n^2 - n}{2} 0 \times {}^{n-2} + \text{etc.}$$

Let now the increments vanish, and their last proportion will be 1 to nx^{n-1}: hence the fluxion of the quantity x is to the fluxion of the quantity x^n as 1: nx^{n-1}. The fluxion of lines, straight or curved, in all cases whatever, as also the fluxions of superficies, angles, and other quantities, can be obtained in the same manner by the method of prime and ultimate ratios. But to establish in this way the analysis of infinite quantities, and to investigate prime and ultimate ratios of finite quantities, nascent or evanescent, is in harmony with the geometry of the ancients; and I have endeavored to show that, in the method of fluxions, it is not necessary to introduce into geometry infinitely small quantities" (quoted in Cajori, *op. cit.*, p. 198). Cajori points out that when 0 (which here is an infinitesimal) becomes nothing, the ratio

$$\frac{0}{0} = nx^{n-1},$$

which needs further elucidation. This method had met with difficulties and objections (Cajori, pp. 198-199). For this reason, Novalis claims that the main difficulty of this calculus resides in the "proportionelle Einteilung" of the differential, *i.e.*, in the ratios and proportions involved in Newton's definition. The difficulty is further emphasized by George Berkeley's claim in the *Analyst* (1734) that the fundamental idea of supposing a finite ratio to exist between terms absolutely evanescent – "the ghosts of departed quantities," as he called them – was absurd and unintelligible (Cajori, p. 219). Leibniz failed to clarify the ratio of the infinitesimals, so did Euler in his *Institutiones Calculi Differentialis*. However, Euler's work further illuminates Novalis' assertion that the main difficulty of the calculus lies in the "proportionelle Einteilung" of the differential. Euler regards the infinitesimal calculus as the study of the ratios of infinitesimals: "In der Infinitesimalrechnung tut man aber nichts anderes, als dass man sich mit der Untersuchung des geometrischen Verhältnisses zwischen verschiedenen unendlich kleinen Grössen beschäftigt, und dabei würde man in die grösste Verwirrung geraten, wofern man nicht diese unendlich kleinen Grössen mit verschiedenen Zeichen bezeichnete" (*Inst. Calc.Diff.*, Michelsen's translation, p. 81). Euler equates infinitesimals to zero, but resists their designation by the symbol of zero, in order to be able to distinguish between various infinitesimals on the one hand, and between the infinitesimals and actual zeros. We quote Euler in greater detail:

Eine unendlich kleine Grösse aber ist nichts anderes als eine verschwindende Grösse, und folglich in der Tat 0. Diese Erklärung des unendlich Kleinen stimmt auch mit der überein, wenn man darunter Grössen versteht, die kleiner sind als jede Grösse, die sich angeben lässt. Denn wenn eine Grösse kleiner ist als jede Grösse, die sich angeben lässt, so muss sie notwendig 0 sein; weil sich, wenn sie es nicht wäre, eine andere ihr gleiche Grösse angeben liesse, welches wider die Voraussetzung streitet. Wir beantworten daher die Frage, was eine unendlich kleine Grösse in der Tat sei, auf die Art, dass wir sagen, sie sei in der Tat 0; und dieser Begriff enthält keins von den grossen Geheimnissen, welche man gemeiniglich in ihm findet, und wodurch man sich verleiten lässt, wider die ganze Rechnung des unendlich Kleinen einen Verdacht zu fassen. Sollten indes einige Zweifel stattfinden, so werden solche in der Folge, wenn wir die Rechnung vortragen werden, gänzlich gehoben werden.

(Euler, *Inst. Calc. Diff.*, Michelsen's transl., I, 79-80).

Thus Euler is convinced in this work that equating infinitesimals to zero would solve the difficulties of calculus. However, regarding all infinitesimals as absolute zeros, and yet realizing the inequality of the infinitesimals relative to each other, compels Euler to introduce his famous distinction between various zeros:

Da wir also gezeigt haben, dass eine unendlich kleine Grösse wirklich Null ist, so müssen wir vor allen Dingen dem Vorwurfe begegnen, warum wir die unendlich kleinen Grössen nicht beständig mit dem Zeichen 0 bezeichnen, sondern dazu besondere Zeichen gebrauchen. Denn da alle Nullen einander gleich sind, so scheint es überflüssig, dass man sich zu ihrer Bezeichnung verschiedener Zeichen bedient. Allein obgleich jede zwei Nullen einander gleich sind, so dass sich zwischen ihnen gar keine Differenz findet: so gibt es doch zwei Arten der Vergleichung der Grössen, wovon die eine die arithmetische und die andere die geometrische ist. Bei jener sehen wir auf die Differenz, bei dieser auf den Quotienten, der aus der Vergleichung der Grössen entspringt; und obgleich das arithmetische Verhältnis zwischen jeden zweien Nullen gleich ist, so ist es deswegen doch das geometrische nicht. Man sieht dies sehr deutlich an dieser geometrischen Proportion, $2 : 1 = 0 : 0$, worin das vierte Glied eben sowohl 0 ist als das dritte. Aber wegen der Natur der Proportion muss, da das erste Glied doppelt so gross ist als das zweite, das dritte Glied auch doppelt so gross sein als das vierte. Dies ist auch selbst aus der gemeinen Arithmetik einleuchtend. Denn da, wie jeder weiss, die Null, mit irgendeiner Zahl multipliziert, wieder Null gibt, oder $n.0 = 0$, und also $n : 1 = 0 : 0$ ist: so fällt daraus in die Augen, dass zwei Nullen, ob sie gleich, arithmetisch betrachtet, in dem Verhältnisse der Gleichheit stehen, dennoch dieses geometrische Verhältnis nicht gegen einander haben. Da also die Nullen jedes Verhältnis zueinander haben können, so bedient man sich, um diese Verschiedenheit anzuzeigen, mit Recht verschiedener Zeichen, zumal, wenn man das geometrische Verhältnis, welches zwischen ihnen statt findet, untersuchen soll. (*Ibid.*, 80-81).

Euler's discussion of proportions involving zeros already met with criticism toward the end of the eighteenth century. But since Euler, as we just saw, defined calculus as the study of the ratios of zeros, *i.e.*, infinitesimals, it is understandable why Novalis regarded "die proportionelle Einteilung" of the differential as the principal puzzle of infinitesimal calculus.

Novalis' definition of calculus is semantic. In modern mathematics this type of definition is looked upon with suspicion. Yet despite all formalization, streamlining, and re-defining of mathematics in recent times, one cannot altogether deny the appropriateness of the term "infinitesimal calculus." In a different context, we have already discussed the following sentence from Novalis' fragments: "Infinitesimalkalkül heisst eigentlich Rechnung, Einteilung oder Messung des Nichteingeteilten – Nichtvergleichbaren – Unermesslichen." Infinitesimal calculus literally means calculus, subdividing or measuring of the indivisible, incommensurate, immeasurable. No matter how diligently Euler had tried to compare, subdivide, and measure the various zeros, Novalis had doubts about this procedure and felt impelled to investigate the relation between various proportions involving ill-defined entities like infinity and infinitesimals. Not unlike Euler, Novalis sets up proportions involving infinity (∞) and infinitesimals $\left(\dfrac{1}{\infty}\right)$:

$$\left(1 \times \infty : 1 :: 1 : \frac{1}{\infty}\right)$$

$$(2 \times \infty) : 1 :: 2 : \frac{1}{\infty}$$

(III, 102)

One of Euler's comments on such proportions may be regarded as a commentary on the specific proportions of Novalis just quoted: "Da sich also geometrisch die unendlich kleine Grösse zur endlichen verhält, wie die endliche Grösse zur unendlich grossen: so muss die endliche Grösse eben so unendlichmal grösser sein als die unendlich kleine, wie die unendliche Grösse unendlich mal grösser ist als die endliche. An dergleichen Redensarten muss man sich nicht stossen, wie viele tun, denn sie beruhen auf den festesten Gründen" (*Inst. Calc. Diff.*, Michelsen's transl., I, 86). It can be readily verified that the two proportions given by Novalis hold, if we operate with the sign ∞ as was done in the eighteenth century, and do not introduce various orders of infinity or apply the limiting process employed in modern mathematics.

Then Novalis introduces what he calls the fundamental formula of infinitesimal calculus: "Die Grundformel des Infinitesimalkalküls:

$$\frac{a}{\infty} \cdot \infty = a \text{ ''}$$

(III, 37).

Haering (p. 551) interprets this formula as follows: "d. h. jede Grösse ist gleich einer unendlichen Summe unendlich kleiner Teile derselben." This interpretation is acceptable if we bear in mind that during Novalis' time no distinction was generally made between various orders of infinity. Novalis' formula

$$\frac{a}{\infty} \cdot \infty = a$$

is a special case of the expression

$$\lim_{x \to \infty} \left(\frac{a}{x} \cdot x\right),$$

namely, the case, where both x's tend to infinity of the same order. The expression may also approach zero or infinity, depending on whether the first or the second x approaches infinity of a higher order. This fact is also partially confirmed by Euler: "Es lässt sich leicht zeigen, dass das Produkt aus einer unendlich grossen und einer unendlich kleinen Grösse nicht bloss eine endliche Grösse, wie schon vorher angemerkt worden ist, sondern auch eine unendlich grosse und eine unendlich kleine Grösse sein kann. Wenn z. B. die unendliche Grösse $\frac{a}{dx}$ [note that to Euler dx equals zero] durch die unendlich kleine Grösse dx multipliziert wird, so ist das Produkt eine endliche Grösse $= a$; wenn aber $\frac{a}{dx}$ durch dx^2 oder dx^3 oder ein anderes unendlich kleines von einer höheren Ordnung multipliziert wird, so ist das Produkt entweder adx, oder adx^2, oder adx^3 etc. und also unendlich klein" (*Inst. Calc. Diff.*, Michelsen's transl., I, 90). Let us read another passage from Euler's *Institutiones Calculi Differentialis* in support of our claim that Novalis' manipulation of zeros and infinity is in line with the mathematical procedures of some of the great, and many lesser, mathematicians of the eighteenth century: "Da also das Zeichen ∞ eine unendlich grosse Grösse bedeutet, so hat man daher die Gleichung, $\frac{a}{dx} = \infty$, deren Richtigkeit auch daraus erhellt, weil man durch die Umkehrung $\frac{a}{\infty} = dx = 0$ erhält" (*Ibid.*, I, 84-85).

In Chapter II, Section 3 we have already discussed Novalis' questions "Gibt es eine Erfindungskunst ohne Data, eine absolute Erfindungskunst?" and "Gibt es eine Rechnung des Unendlichen?" as variants of Kant's fundamental question of pure reason whether synthetic *a priori* judgments are possible. Novalis' latter question is also justified in view of the state of calculus in the eighteenth century.

Novalis extends calculus beyond the strictly mathematical domain in a manner similar to his extension of geometry, arithmetic, and algebra: "Der Differentialkalkül scheint mir die allgemeine Methode, das Unregelmässige auf das Regelmässige zu reduzieren

– es durch eine Funktion des Regelmässigen auszudrücken – es mit dem Regelmässigen zu verbinden – das Regelmässige zu dessen Meter zu machen – es mit demselben zu logarithmisieren" (III, 252). Using the predicate or attribute "infinite" in various associations, Novalis gropes for a "philosophical calculus": "Der unendlich verdünnten Kraft entspricht der unendlich einfache Stoff – und die unendlich lange Auflösungszeit. Der unendlich einfache Stoff ist auch der unendlich kleine Stoff – der Punkt – die unendlich dünne Kraft ist auch die unbegrenzte, das ist ungegliederte Kraft oder reine Bewegung – der Weltraum des Chaos – die unendlich lange Auflösungszeit ist die Ewigkeit ante – die Weltzeit des Chaos. Philosophischer Differential- und Integralkalkül" (III, 177-178). The entire method of abstraction, so common in philosophy, bears a striking resemblance to calculus: "Der Abstraktionskalkül der Philosophie ist vollkommen dem Infinitesimalkalkül zu vergleichen" (III, 156). Novalis is fully aware of his use of calculus in contexts deviating from the usual. For example, after applying some of the criteria of calculus to history, he remarks: "Integration und Differentiation nehme ich hier nicht ganz in der gewöhnlichen Bedeutung" (III, 243).

We must remember, as we read Novalis' reflections on calculus, that they are momentary flashes in his mind hastily jotted down, to be revised and partially discarded before using them in his universal encyclopedia.

Function, Continuity, Infinity. Novalis' fragments on these concepts are discussed in detail by Hamburger (128ff.). The reader is referred also to the summary of her views in Chapter I, Section 3 of this book. We will therefore not take them up again in this section. Novalis' concept of infinity is touched upon throughout the present study. Its relevance in literary criticism is taken up in the next chapter, in the section entitled "Mathematics and Literature."

CHAPTER IV

NOVALIS' FRAGMENTS ON MATHEMATICS, PART TWO MATHEMATICAL CONCEPTS PROJECTED INTO FIELDS OF KNOWLEDGE OTHER THAN THE PHYSICAL SCIENCES

> Alle Wissenschaften sollen Mathematik werden. Die bisherige Mathematik ist nur die erste und leichteste Äusserung oder Offenbarung des wahrhaft wissenschaftlichen Geistes (III, 18).
>
> NOVALIS

1. MATHEMATICS AS THE IDEAL SCIENCE AND THE BASIS FOR A UNIVERSAL ENCYCLOPEDIA OF KNOWLEDGE

In the preceding chapters we have already alluded to Novalis' grand aim of unifying all branches of knowledge in a universal encyclopedia using mathematics as a linking principle. We also saw how Novalis tries to give meaning to mathematical distinctions outside the proper realm of the various branches of mathematics. In this chapter, we shall first consider what properties of mathematics made Novalis set this science above all others. Then we will examine his application of mathematical concepts to various branches of knowledge.

Novalis' preoccupation with an encyclopedia of knowledge is rooted in the period in which he lived. During the eighteenth century many encyclopedias were planned and published, notably the French *Encyclopédie* (see Haering, pp. 57ff.). This encyclopedia proclaimed the advent of the age of science and placed great emphasis on mathematics. In fact, one of its most prominent editors was the mathematician d'Alembert.

Why did Novalis elect mathematics as the guiding and normative principle for his encyclopedia? Mathematicians were the only ones, Novalis contends, who had revealed a truly scientific spirit in their endeavors. "Echter wissenschaftlicher Geist hat vorzüglich bisher bei den Mathematikern geherrscht" (III, 248). Therefore all sciences are to become mathematics: "Alle Wissenschaften sollen Mathematik werden. Die bisherige Mathematik ist nur die erste und leichteste Äusserung oder Offenbarung des wahrhaft wissenschaftlichen Geistes" (III, 18). An essential requirement for a universal encyclopedia is an ordering principle. Novalis holds that the mathematical "force" is an ordering force: "Die mathematische Kraft ist die ordnende Kraft" (III, 257). To reduce to order is to classify, categorize, and organize. These activities require a capacity of acute discernment, which, in its turn, is based on a faculty of perceiving differences. This latter ability is, according to Novalis, mathematical: "Wären wir nicht von Grund auf mathematisch, so nähmen wir gar keine Unterschiede etc. wahr" (III, 160). Our very thinking process is mathematical: "Rechnen und Denken ist eins. Soviel Denkhandlungen – und soviel Zusammensetzungen derselben, soviel Rechnungsarten. Nur unvollkommenes Rechnen ist vom Denken überhaupt verschieden – so wie das unvollkommene und besondere Denken vom Denken überhaupt" (III, 24). The application of mathematics to our thinking process is further explored in the following fragment: "*Mathematische Logik.* Anwendung der Mathematik auf die Denklehre – Schnelligkeit – und Reichhaltigkeit des Denkens – nicht auch Stärke des Denkens. Grade des Denkens. Die Sprache ist ein Gedankenmeter. Scharfes Denken – eindringliches Denken" (III, 198). Or again: "Man bildet das Auge und die Denkkraft mathematisch – der Geist rechnet aus den durch das Auge ihm kritisch gegebenen Datis – nach Regeln der Reduktion der perspektivischen Ansicht – die wahre Grösse, Gestalt, Kraft etc. und die Entfernung des Gegenstandes" (III, 195).

Perhaps mathematics is not just a science in the usual sense, but a universal scientific tool, human reason objectified and embodied in an outward form: "Am Ende ist die ganze Mathematik gar keine besondere Wissenschaft, sondern nur ein allgemein wissenschaftliches Werkzeug – ein schönes Werkzeug ist eine contradictio in adjecto. Sie ist vielleicht nichts als die exoterisierte, zu einem äusseren Objekt und Organ gemachte Seelenkraft des Verstandes, ein realisierter und objektivisierter Verstand" (III, 71).

Novalis' glorification of mathematics as a science culminates in some of his so-called "hymns to mathematics":

> Die ganze Mathematik ist eigentlich eine Gleichung im grossen für die anderen Wissenschaften.
> Was ihr die Logarithmen sind, das ist sie den anderen Wissenschaften.
> Der Begriff der Mathematik ist der Begriff der Wissenschaft überhaupt.
> Alle Wissenschaften sollen daher Mathematik werden.
> Die jetzige Mathematik ist wenig mehr als ein speziell empirisches Organon.
> Sie ist eine Substitution zur bequemeren Reduktion – ein Hülfsmittel des Denkens.

Ihre vollständige Anwendbarkeit ist ein notwendiges Postulat ihres Begriffs.
Die reine Mathematik ist die Anschauung des Verstandes als Universum.
Die höhere Mathematik enthält am Ende nur Abkürzungsmethoden. (III, 295-296).

Some of Novalis' fragments deal with the usual applications of mathematics to nature and the natural sciences. Nature constantly adds, subtracts, etc.: "Die Natur addiert, subtrahiert, multipliziert, potenziert etc. unaufhörlich. Die angew[andten] mathematischen Wissenschaften zeigen uns die Natur als Mathematiker. Die reale Mathematik ist die Physik" (II, 19). More specifically, he defines various branches of knowledge as specific types of mathematics: "Die Mathematik der Kräfte ist die Mechanik. Die Mathematik der Gestalten ist die Geometrie. Die Mathematik des Lichts ist die Optik. Die Mathematik des Ohrs ist der Generalbass. Die Mathematik des Gesichts – die Perspektive" (III, 17).

Other fragments of Novalis deal with more unusual applications of mathematics. Mathematics is to him an axis, about which most branches of knowledge revolve. He writes:

Poetik der Mathematik.
Grammatik der Mathematik.
Physik der Mathematik.
Philosophie der Mathematik.

Mathematik der Philosophie.
Mathematik der Natur.
Mathematik der Poesie.
Mathematik der Geschichte.
Mathematik der Mathematik. (III, 19).

A possible order of the process of mathematization is suggested by the following fragments of Novalis: "Jede mathematische Wissenschaft strebt wieder philosophisch zu werden – animiert oder rationalisiert zu werden – dann poetisch – endlich moralisch – zuletzt religiös" (III, 257).

2. MATHEMATICS AND PHILOSOPHY

The basic idea in Novalis' thought on the interrelations of mathematics and philosophy is that they should approximate each other. Conventional mathematics should be freed from the yoke of excessive rigor; conventional philosophy, from the extremes of arbitrariness and dogma. Of the non-physical fields of knowledge, philosophy is the first to be mathematized. Once philosophy has been mathematized, the basic distinction between mathematics and philosophy will cease to exist; mathematics and philosophy merge into a universal science. If then the process of mathematizing other branches of knowledge is continued, it is no longer necessary to state explicitly whether the new branch of knowledge is to be mathematized or philosophized. Hence there is no contradiction between those of Novalis' fragments, according to which all knowledge is to be mathematized, and those fragments, according to which it is to be philosophized. At the beginning of the process of mathematization the order of precedence is mathematics over philosophy, but as soon as mathematics and philosophy are one science, the next branch of knowledge is either philosophized or mathematized, or both.

Novalis states: "Am Ende ist Mathematik nur gemeine, einfache Philosophie und Philosophie höhere Mathematik im allgemeinen" (III, 193). Perhaps mathematics is common philosophy, and philosophy higher mathematics, Novalis states. At any rate, many analogies between them may be pointed out: "Höhere Mathematik und Philosophie (oder Theorie der Ideen, des Unendlichen etc.) haben sehr viel Analogie (Kurven – Reihen) Elemente. Drei Achsen" (II, 378). Novalis continues to explore the various ways in which mathematics and philosophy overlap. Both philosophy and mathematics are concerned with syntheses based on arbitrary assumptions: "Die Philosophie ist, wie alle synthetische Wissenschaft, wie die Mathematik, willkürlich" (III, 342). Yet true philosophy, and hence mathematics, must be a play of ideas of the utmost regularity: "Das regelmässigste Ideenspiel ist die wahre Philosophie" (II, 131). Novalis considers all possible relations between philosophy and mathematics. Is philosophy the result of reflecting on mathematics? Is it the animating principle of mathematics, or, using the ancient Aristotelian distinction, is philosophy matter, and mathematics its form? "Sollte die Philosophie überhaupt aus der Reflexion über die Mathematik entstehen? – Philosophie ist die Universal- oder höhere Mathematik, das belebende Prinzip der Mathematik, die poetische Mathematik. Oder der Stoff, wenn die Mathematik die Form ist" (III, 137). General propositions of philosophy correspond to algebraic formulae: "Allgemeine Sätze sind nichts als algebraische Formeln. Die reine Philosophie ist daher gerade so etwas wie die Lettern-Algebra. So eine Formel kann ein Gattungs-, ein Klassen-, und Lokalzeichen sein" (II, 383). Sometimes Novalis wonders whether there is such a thing as a concrete science of philosophy. Only mathematics and physics are concrete sciences, and philosophy is perhaps, like the philosopher's stone or the squaring of the circle, a "necessary" yet unattainable goal of scientists: "Es gibt keine Philosophie in concreto. Philosophie ist wie der Stein der Weisen, die Quadratur des Zirkels usw. eine blosse notwendige Aufgabe der Szientifiker, das Ideal der Wissenschaft überhaupt. ...Es gibt, als konkrete Wissenschaften, nur Mathematik und Physik. Philosophie ist die Intelligenz selbst; vollendete Philosophie ist vollendete Intelligenz" (III, 228). Another possibility of associating mathematics and philosophy is given by the categories: "*Mathematische Philosophie (Grammatik)*. Die Kategorien sind das Alphabet cogitationum humanarum – worin jeder Buchstabe eine Handlung begreift – eine philosophische Operation – einen höheren (mathematischen) Kalkül. – Die Philosophie der Kategorien ist von der höchsten Wichtigkeit" (III, 98).

Of the more specific philosophical problems, to which Novalis applies the critical apparatus of mathematics, we already discussed the dialectic method and the system of categories (see Chapter II). Hamburger (pp. 177 ff.) already dealt with Novalis' conception of time and space, in which she perceives an adumbration of the theory of relativity.

Novalis deals with another important philosophical problem in the light of the combination of signs in ordinary algebra and arithmetic: the problem of the interrelations of truth and falsity. "Wahrhafte Darstellung des Irrtums ist indirekte Darstellung der Wahrheit. Wahrhafte Darstellung der Wahrheit ist allein wahrhaft. Wahrhafte Darstellung des Irrtums ist zum Teil selbst Irrtum. Entgegengesetzte irrige Darstellung des Irrtums gibt Wahrheit.

$$- \times - = + \quad | \quad + \times + = +$$
$$+ \times - = - \quad | \quad - \times + = -."$$
(III, 225).

The minus sign here stands for falsity or error, the plus sign for truth, the multiplication sign, for "representation of." In this manner Novalis translates the rules of signs successively into the following propositions: (1) an erroneous representation of error may give rise to a true statement; (2) a true representation of error or falsity reveals this error or falsity; (3) a true representation of truth yields truth; (4) a false representation of truth is a falsity.

3. MATHEMATICS AND MAGIC

Since Heinrich Simon's study *Der magische Idealismus* (see Chapter I, Section 3) literary critics have designated Novalis' philosophy as "magic idealism," a designation regarded as paradoxical by Nikolai Hartmann (*Die Philosophie des deutschen Idealismus*, Berlin & Leipzig, 1923, I, 225), and as misleading by Haering (p. 364). The term was introduced by Novalis himself (III, 110, 227).

Magic idealism, as Novalis conceives it, strives for the primacy and dominion of the spiritual over the physical world. The magic idealist is not content with merely according to the world of the spirit a higher valuation than the world of matter. The spiritual world is created by the Ego in the Fichtean sense. The physical world may, through the magic idealism, not only be subjected to, but re-shaped and molded to fit into the ideal, spiritual universe. The human body is part of the physical world. The mastery over the former is the initial stage of the mastery over the latter. In some future epoch of magic, body will be subservient to the soul: "In dieser Periode der Magie dient der Körper der Seele, oder der Geisterwelt" (II, 336). Thus the physical world is subjected to the spiritual. The spiritual, in its turn, is guided by the human will: "Die Welt hat eine ursprüngliche Fähigkeit durch mich belebt zu werden – Sie ist überhaupt a priori von mir belebt – eins mit mir. Ich habe eine ursprüngliche Tendenz und Fähigkeit die Welt zu beleben – Nun kann ich aber mit nichts in Verhältnis treten – was sich nicht nach meinem Willen richtet oder ihm gemäss ist – Mithin muss die Welt die ursprüngliche Anlage haben sich nach mir zu richten – meinem Willen gemäss zu sein" (II, 343). In short, magic is to Novalis the art of the arbitrary use of the world of sense perception: "Magie ist = Kunst, die Sinnenwelt willkürlich zu gebrauchen" (II, 336).

Thus physical nature is to be subjected to the spirit by magic. But all branches of knowledge dealing with the spiritual and physical universe are to be mathematized. Hence mathematics and magic shall, Novalis contends, ultimately serve the same purpose: "Echte Mathematik ist das eigentliche Element des Magiers" (III, 295). For this reason Novalis regards the question "Ist Magie möglich?" (III, 231) as a valid variant of Kant's question whether pure mathematics is possible (see Chapter II, Section 3).

4. MATHEMATICS AND RELIGION

Novalis seeks a "coincidentia oppositorum" of science and dogma. These extremes must not exclude, but should supplement each other: "Wissenschaft ist nur eine Hälfte, Glauben ist die andere" (II, 217). Belief, or dogma, is the beginning and end of knowledge, or science: "Alles Wissen endigt und fängt im Glauben an" (III, 216). Science is embedded in the realm of belief. Hence an extension of science would widen the realm of belief: "Vor- und Rückerweiterung des Wissens ist Hinausschiebung – Erweiterung des Glaubensgebiets" (III, 217). The purest form of science is mathematics. The purest form of dogma is religion. Consequently, a reconciliation of science and dogma could best be achieved by a fusion of mathematics and

religion. In anticipation of such a fusion, Novalis calls his intended universal encyclopedia of knowledge a "szientifische Bibel" (III, 208) and boldly links various religious concepts with mathematics in his hymns to mathematics:
> Das Leben der Götter ist Mathematik.
> Alle göttlichen Gesandten müssen Mathematiker sein.
> Reine Mathematik ist Religion.
> Zur Mathematik gelangt man nur durch eine Theophanie.
> Wer ein mathematisches Buch nicht mit Andacht ergreift, und es wie Gottes Wort liest, der versteht es nicht. (III, 296).

In fact, according to Novalis, there is no reason why God could not manifest himself through mathematics: "Kann sich Gott nicht auch in der Mathematik offenbaren wie in jeder anderen Wissenschaft?" (III, 337).

5. MATHEMATICS AND LANGUAGE

In three spheres of meaning Novalis points out analogies between mathematics and language: (1) symbolism, (2) grammar, (3) logic.

Before analyzing the meaning of linguistic and mathematical symbols, Novalis dwells rhapsodically on their self-sufficient, abstract form, on the complete independence of the latter from their content. "Wenn man den Leuten nur begreiflich machen könnte, dass es mit der Sprache wie mit den mathematischen Formeln sei – Sie machen eine Welt für sich aus – Sie spielen nur mit sich selbst, drücken nichts als ihre wunderbare Natur aus, und eben darum sind sie so ausdrucksvoll – eben darum spiegelt sich in ihnen das seltsame Verhältnisspiel der Dinge" (II, 230-231). Pure, abstract language and mathematics are mere symbols and thought processes. These symbols are arbitrarily selected, then dogmatically used as instruments for our mental operations: "Reine Mathematik hat nichts mit Grösse zu tun. Sie ist blosse Bezeichnungslehre – mechanisch gewordener, in Verhältnissen geordneter Gedankenoperationen. Sie muss lediglich willkürlich-dogmatisch instrumental sein. – So auf ähnliche Weise ist es auch mit der abstrakten Sprache" (III, 325). Kant holds that a body of empirical knowledge may be elevated to a science only if this knowledge may be reconstructed *a priori* from arbitrary assumptions. Realizing that mathematics is based on arbitrary assumptions, Novalis wishes to satisfy himself that language is of similar origin. The more analogies between mathematics and language he is able to discover, the easier it will be for him to mathematize language for his projected encyclopedia. He notes in one of his fragments: "Erfindung der Sprache a priori" (III, 246), but is more explicit in another fragment: "Die Sprache und die Sprachzeichen sind a priori aus der menschlichen Natur entsprungen, und die ursprüngliche Sprache war echt wissenschaftlich – Sie wiederaufzufinden ist der Zweck des Grammatikers" (III, 259). In the beginning, men agreed that certain symbols would stand for certain things. In this manner, language was constructed, not unlike mathematics: "Die ganze Sprache ist ein Postulat. Sie ist positiven, freien Ursprungs. Man musste sich einverstehen, bei gewissen Zeichen gewisse Dinge zu denken, mit Absicht etwas Bestimmtes in sich zu konstruieren" (II, 347).

Having considered the similarities of mathematical and linguistic symbols, Novalis proceeds to point out the analogies between the respective systems of these symbols. The system of numbers is a model for a genuine system of linguistic symbols. Numbers shall become letters, and language is to become arithmetic: "Das Zahlensystem ist Muster eines echten Sprachzeichensystems – Unsere Buchstaben sollen Zahlen, unsere Sprache Arithmetik werden" (III, 18). A further comparison of the structure of mathematics and language inevitably leads to a consideration of grammar and logic. One of Novalis' fragments, bearing the heading *"Mathematik und Grammatik,"* reads: "Über die Logarithmen – die eigentliche Sprache ist ein Logarithmensystem" (III, 228). Logarithms had been invented by Napier about two hundred years before Novalis studied mathematics. Logarithms had enabled mathematicians to carry out elementary arithmetical operations much quicker than by the usual processes. In the fragment just quoted Novalis suggests that the ideal, proper language would resemble a system of logarithms in its capacity of simplifying and accelerating mental processes. An indirect approach to the mathematization of language is indicated by Novalis' note "Grammatik der Mathematik" (III, 19).

The final union of mathematics and language is to be effected through logic. We already saw that to Novalis mathematics is the objectification and embodiment of human reason (cf. Section 1). By describing logic as the grammar of our thought, the functions of mathematics and logic coincide: "Die gewöhnliche Logik ist die Grammatik der höheren Sprache oder des Denkens. Sie enthält bloss die Verhältnisse der Begriffe untereinander" (II, 321). Another fragment confirms this argument: *"Mathematische Logik.* Anwendung der Mathematik auf die Denklehre – Schnelligkeit – und Reichhaltigkeit des Denkens – nicht auch Stärke des Denkens. Grade des Denkens. Die Sprache ist ein Gedankenmeter" (III, 198).

It should be noted, although it cannot be dealt with, here that Novalis' preoccupation with mathematics is reflected in his fragments by a metaphorical use of mathematical concepts and symbols (see also H. Fauteck, *Die Sprachtheorie Friedrich von Hardenbergs*, Berlin, 1940).

6. MATHEMATICS AND LITERATURE

Like other early German Romanticists, as for example, Friedrich Schlegel, and, to a lesser extent, August Wilhelm Schlegel, Novalis employs mathematical concepts and symbols in his fragments dealing with literary criticism. As a German Romanticist, he concerns himself frequently with the novel, *i.e.*, the literary genre which was elevated by the Romanticists from the level of second-rate literature to that of the lofty precincts of poetry and drama. The novel is usually regarded as the successor to the epic. In this connection Novalis states in the following fragment: "Das epische Gedicht ist das veredelte primitive Gedicht. Im wesentlichen ganz dasselbe. Der Roman steht schon weit höher – jenes dauert fort – dieser wächst fort – in jenem ist arithmetische, im Roman geometrische Progression" (II, 326). The essential difference between the epic and the novel lies in the pace. The epic is characterized by a steady pace, by duration; the novel, by a quickened pace, or, inversely, a retarded pace, by development and growth. The steady pace may be very adequately represented by an arithmetical progression, in which the difference between any two adjacent terms is the same, *i.e.*,

$$a, a + d, a + 2d, a + 3d, \ldots$$

or, using numbers,

$$3, 5, 7, 9, 11, \ldots$$

The accelerated, or retarded, pace may be best illustrated by a geometric progression, in which the difference between any two adjacent terms varies with the position of the terms in the progression, in which, however, the ratio of any two adjacent terms is constant. For example,

$$a, ac, ac^2, ac^3, ac^4, \ldots$$

If the factor c is an improper fraction, or greater than 1, the terms increase, *i.e.*, the pace is accelerated. If the factor c is a proper fraction, or less than 1, the terms decrease, *i.e.*, the pace is slowed.

As an example of an epic one is reminded of the *Iliad* with its steady flow of events. An example of a novel with a slowed pace is Thomas Mann's *Zauberberg*, in which each of the seven chapters is longer than the preceding, both in duration and page length. Acceleration and retardation are thus associated with the crucial early Romantic concept of progression. A number of other fragments of Novalis deal with progression as a basic characteristic of the novel. For example: "Darstellung eines Gegenstandes in Reihen (Variationsreihen – Abänderungen, etc.) So z.B. die Personendarstellung in 'Meister,' die schöne Seele und Natalie – bei der Selbstreflexion – bei den Dingen der ersten, zweiten, dritten Hand etc. So ist z. B. eine historische Reihe, eine Sammlung Kupferstiche vom rohsten Anfang der Kunst bis zur Vollendung und so fort – der Formen vom Frosch bis zum Apollo etc." (II, 410-411). In another fragment the novel is compared to an infinite series: "Alle Zufälle unseres Lebens sind Materialien, aus denen wir machen können, was wir wollen. Wer viel Geist hat, macht viel aus seinem Leben. Jede Bekanntschaft, jeder Vorfall, wäre für den durchaus Geistigen erstes Glied einer unendlichen Reihe, Anfang eines unendlichen Romans" (II, 25). By saying "im Roman ist geometrische Progression" Novalis touches on several important interrelated concepts of the early Romantic theory of literature, namely, "Reihe," infinity, "Potenz." These terms are conceptually linked in two frames of reference: (1) in early Romantic theory of literature; (2) mathematically, since each may mathematically be defined in terms of the other two. The concept of progression, "Reihe," is intimately associated with the concept "progressiv." The mathematical concept of progression is reflected in the following fragment: "Roman – wohlgeordnete, gesetzmässige Reihe" (II, 366). In another fragment progression is linked with variation, a notion with which the combinatorial school of mathematics was obsessed: "Darstellung eines Gegenstandes in Reihen (Variationsreihen – Abänderungen etc.) So z. B. die Personendarstellung im 'Meister,' die schöne Seele und Natalie – bei der Selbstreflexion – bei den Dingen der ersten, zweiten, dritten Hand etc." (II, 410f.). The term and concept of "progressiv" appears also in Friedrich Schlegel's definitive pronouncement on the nature of Romantic literature: "Die romantische Poesie ist eine progressive Universalpoesie" (*Athenäum*, 1. Bd., 2. St., p. 28).

In mathematics, infinity is, in general, regarded as the limit of an unending series or sequence, something that may be approached progressively, but may never be reached. Thus one never says "equals infinity," but rather "tends to infinity." Similarly, the concept of progression yields the concept of infinity in early Romantic literary criticism. Novalis' fragments reveal the mathematical basis of the conceptual interrelation of "Reihe" and "Unendlichkeit." We read in one of the fragments: "Jede Grösse kann durch eine Reihe ausgedrückt werden. Ist die Reihe geschlossen, bestimmt, so ist die Grösse bestimmt; ist die Reihe unendlich, so ists auch die Grösse" (III, 23). If we now look again at a fragment already quoted above, we will see the equivalence of the idea of progression toward infinity in mathematics and in the Romantic conception of the novel: "Alle Zufälle unseres Lebens sind Materialien, aus denen wir machen können, was wir wollen. Wer viel Geist hat, macht viel aus seinem Leben. Jede Bekanntschaft, jeder Vorfall, wäre für den durchaus Geistigen erstes Glied einer unendlichen Reihe, Anfang eines unendlichen Romans" (II, 25). Progression tending to infinity expresses the Romantic idea of growth and development, "das Werdende." Again, the latter term is employed by Novalis in a more strictly mathematical context: "Unendliche Grössen sind werdende Grössen, Approximationen an Grössen" (III, 21). We recall in this connection Friedrich Schlegel's observation: "Die romantische Dichtkunst ist noch im Werden; ja, das ist ihr eigentlichstes Wesen, dass sie ewig nur werden, nie vollendet sein kann" (*Athenäum*, 1. Bd., 2. St., p. 70). The synonymity, at least partial, of "Werden" and "progressiv" is confirmed, for example, by Kluckhohn's interpretation of the latter as "dauernd fortschreitend in der Annäherung an das Unendliche" (*Das Ideengut der deutschen Romantik*, 3. Aufl., Tübingen, 1953, p. 184).

The third term in the closely linked triad, of which "Reihe" and infinity formed the first two, is "Potenz." Not only may a progression approach infinity horizontally, as it were, in an unending sequence of terms, but each term itself tends to infinity through "Potenz," in a vertical direction, as you go on in the progression. If we recall Novalis' formulation "Roman ist geometrische Reihe" and bear in mind that a geometric progression is a sequence of "Potenzen," *i.e.*, of terms with ascending powers, the connection becomes clear. Friedrich Schlegel says of Romantic poetry: "... [sie kann] ... frei von allem realen und idealen Interesse auf den Flügeln der poetischen Reflexion in der Mitte schweben, diese Reflexion immer wieder potenzieren und wie in einer endlosen Reihe von Spiegeln vervielfachen" (*Ath.*, 1. Bd., 2. St., p. 29). Thus the term "Potenzreihe" and other associated terms become more comprehensible in Novalis' definitive pronouncement on Romantic literature: "Die Welt muss romantisiert werden. So findet man den ursprünglichen Sinn wieder. Romantisieren ist nichts als eine qualitative Potenzierung. Das niedre Selbst wird mit einem bessern Selbst in dieser Operation identifiziert. So wie wir selbst eine solche qualitative Potenzreihe sind. Diese Operation ist noch ganz unbekannt. Indem ich dem Gemeinen einen hohen Sinn, dem Gewöhnlichen ein geheimnisvolles Ansehn, dem Bekannten die Würde des Unbekannten, dem Endlichen einen unendlichen Schein gebe, so romantisiere ich es. – Umgekehrt ist die Operation für das Höhere, Unbekannte, Mystische, Unendliche – dies wird durch diese Verknüpfung logarithmisiert... Wechselerhöhung und Erniedrigung" (II, 335). The terms "Potenzierung," "Potenzreihe," "bekannt" and "unbekannt," "endlich" and "unendlich," "Operation," and "logarithmisieren" are all mathematical and suggest Novalis' projection of mathematical thought patterns into literary criticism.

It is significant that the two principal definitions of early German Romantic literature revolve about terms of mathematical origin. Friedrich Schlegel's frequent use of mathematical symbols, in particular, of power exponents, and their inverse, radical signs, makes the mathematical origin of the terms discussed above unquestionable (see Friedrich Schlegel, *Literary Notebooks* 1797-1801, ed. Hans Eichner, London & Toronto, 1957).

The close relation of Novalis' and Friedrich Schlegel's theories of literary criticism to the combinatorial analysis of the Leipzig mathematician Hindenburg becomes apparent also from other fragments. For example: "Romantisieren, ähnlich dem Algebraisieren" (III, 63). Like the combinatorial analyst, the Romanticist varies and combines ideas. The very skill of Romantic exploration of ideas is tantamount to a capacity for variation and combination, the chief operations of the combinatorial school of mathematics: "Gelehrsamkeit entspricht dem Gedächtnis. Fähigkeit oder Geschicklichkeit dem Geist. Beides verbinden heisst beides als ein Binomium ansehn und dieses potenzieren. (Romantische Gelehrsamkeit – und romantische Geschicklichkeit – **Kombinations- und Variationsfertigkeit**)" (III, 94). The binomial theorem mentioned in this fragment was much discussed by the adherents of the combinatorial school and regarded by some of them as the most important theorem of mathematical analysis.

Next we shall discuss the relation of fragment as a literary genre to the concepts of progression and infinity. Novalis states: "Wenige bekannte Glieder, durch die man instand gesetzt wird, eine unendliche Menge unbekannter Glieder zu finden, machen die Konstruktionsformel einer Reihe aus" (III, 38). If a few terms of a mathematical series or sequence are known, it is possible to produce more and more terms, and it is not necessary, or possible, to write down the entire sequence, since the latter is infinite. Thus a few finite terms, *i.e.*, a fragmentary sequence, indicate the path toward infinity. Similarly, early Romantic fragments are, according to Novalis, "Anfänge interessanter Gedankenfolgen," "literarische Sämereien," "Texte zum Denken," capable of infinite expansion, yet remaining finite, and hence fragmentary. The intentional finiteness manifest in the completeness and conclusiveness of the classical work of literature or art is undesirable to the early German Romanticist, because completion and perfection is achieved at the price of voluntary renunciation of infinity.

A number of Novalis' fragments deal with the affinities of the mathematical and literary creative processes. One of these fragments reads: "Der poetische Philosoph ist en état de Créateur absolu. Ein Kreis, ein Triangel werden schon auf diese Art kreiert. Es kommt ihnen nichts zu, als was der Verfertiger ihnen zukommen lässt etc.

Man muss überhaupt immer bedenken, dass das Höchste, zwar nicht in der wirklichen, aber in der idealischen Geschichte, vor dem Niedrigeren etc. kommt – also auch, wenn der Mathematiker wirklich etwas Richtiges tut, so tut ers als poeta philosophus" (III, 145). As in his fragments on definition (Chapter III, Section 1), Novalis here emphasizes the freedom of mathematical creation. Like the poet, the "maker," the mathematician freely associates elements in accordance with freely chosen rules, and generates structures that may incidentally resemble, but do not essentially represent physical or historical reality. In fact, Novalis even goes so far as to claim: "Die Mathematik ist echte Wissenschaft, weil sie gemachte Kenntnisse enthält" (III, 270). Great mathematicians, when reflecting on the nature of mathematics, have always attested to this. The well-known distichon of the mathematician L. Kronecker may be adduced here in confirmation of our argument: "Wir Mathematiker auch sind echte, berufene Dichter; / Uns liegt noch der Beweis für das Gedichtete ob!" (see the collection by W. Ahrens, *Scherz und Ernst in der Mathematik*. Geflügelte und ungeflügelte Worte, Leipzig, 1904, p. 226).

The question arises whether, beyond his literary criticism, Novalis' meditations on mathematics are reflected in his literary works proper. Indeed, they are, significantly so, though peripherally and indirectly. All of Novalis' prose works are fragmentary, with the exception of the essay *Die Christenheit oder Europa*. Yet all these fragments, the philosophical as well as novelistic, show an orientation toward a Utopian resolution of the conflicts of life, the antitheses of art, the dichotomies of thought. The philosophical fragments adumbrate an ideal union of mathematics, magic, religion, language, literature, the sciences, and all other branches of knowledge in a pattern governed by "arithmetica universalis." His projected universal encyclopedia of knowledge is to be conceived as a step toward that final state of "coincidentia oppositorum." The two novelistic fragments *Die Lehrlinge zu Sais* and *Heinrich von Ofterdingen* mysteriously allude to a higher symbolism in a visionary realm of fairy tale, with the laws of nature rescinded, the law of contradiction repealed, with man and animal, spirits and matter communicating in a universal symbolic language, in short, a golden age, ruled by the poet-priest-magician-musician-mathematician. Thus the teleological vectors of the philosophical and novelistic fragments of Novalis are parallels that meet at infinity.

Die Lehrlinge zu Sais abounds in configurations of universal mathematics. Music and mathematics are linked in the spirit of Pythagoras and Chladni, as music of the spheres and musical figures. "Arithmetica universalis" appears in the following passage: "Dankbar legt der Priester diese neue, erhabene Messkunst auf den

Altar..." (I, 34). In his study *Novalis, Die Lehrlinge zu Sais. Versuch einer Erläuterung* (Winthertur, 1954), Heinz Bollinger recognizes the mathematical echoes in this work of Novalis. Of the "erhabene Messkunst" he correctly says in the light of Novalis' fragments, "die sowohl mit der Mathematik als mit der Dichtkunst wesensverwandt sein muss" (p. 49). A number of other mathematical allusions are established by Bollinger (pp. 2, 12, 13, 15, 19, 42, 44, 53).

Numbers and figures, "Zahlen und Figuren," appear symbolically in all major works of Novalis. The process of transmuting reality into symbols, poetical and mathematical, is depicted in the fairy tale in *Heinrich von Ofterdingen*. The crucial passage is quoted here: "Die Frau wandte sich zuzeiten gegen Ginnistan und die Kinder, tauchte den Finger in die Schale, und sprützte einige Tropfen auf sie hin, die, sobald sie die Amme, das Kind, oder die Wiege berührten, in einen blauen Dunst zerrannen, der tausend seltsame Bilder zeigte, und beständig um sie herzog und sich veränderte. Traf einer davon zufällig auf den Schreiber, so fielen eine Menge Zahlen und geometrische Figuren nieder, die er mit vieler Emsigkeit auf einen Faden zog" (I, 198). There is a contrast in this passage between the more concrete "Bilder" and the more abstract "Zahlen und Figuren." In Novalis' ultimate magical mathematics the two would merge. "Zahlen und Figuren" is frequently employed by Novalis as a stage of mathematics preliminary to higher stages of magical mathematics. In Section 3 of Chapter III we already saw that Novalis regarded algebraic letters as a stage of mathematics closer to "arithmetica universalis," due to the abandonment of "Zahlen und Figuren" for the algebraic letters, which were more inclusive and more universal than the former. A similar interpretation applies to the verses, already quoted in Chapter III, Section 3:

> *Wenn nicht mehr Zahlen und Figuren*
> *Sind Schlüssel aller Kreaturen,*
> *Wenn die, so singen oder küssen,*
> *Mehr als die Tiefgelehrten wissen,*
> *Wenn sich die Welt ins freie Leben,*
> *Und in die Welt wird zurückgegeben,*
> *Wenn dann sich wieder Licht und Schatten*
> *Zu echter Klarheit werden gatten,*
> *Und man in Märchen und Gedichten*
> *Erkennt die ewgen Weltgeschichten,*
> *Dann fliegt vor einem geheimen Wort*
> *Das ganze verkehrte Wesen fort.* (I, 251).

In the progression from ordinary mathematics to magical mathematics, the higher symbolism, the mathematical number yields to the magical numeral, the magic word. An even more arid variant of "Zahlen und Figuren" appears in the gloomy vision of the post- and antemagical state of man in the fifth hymn to the night. It is a vision of the domination of "dürre Zahl und das strenge Mass," and even words cannot conjure up a coherent image, but disintegrate like dust: "Zu Ende neigte die alte Welt sich. Des jungen Geschlechts Lustgarten verwelkte – hinauf in den freieren, wüsten Raum strebten die unkindlichen, wachsenden Menschen. Die Götter verschwanden mit ihrem Gefolge – Einsam und leblos stand die Natur. Mit eiserner Kette band sie die dürre Zahl und das strenge Mass. Wie in Staub und Lüfte zerfiel in dunkle Worte die unermessliche Blüte des Lebens. Entflohn war der beschwörende Glauben, und die allverwandelnde, allverschwisternde Himmelsgenossin, die Phantasie" (I, 61). It is significant that "dürre Zahl" and "dunkle Worte" are here alike in their symbolic power, or rather, in their lack of it with regard to "die unermessliche Blüte des Lebens." We see in this passage also, albeit negatively, Novalis' conception of mathematics and language as symbolic media of the same kind, but of varying degrees of application. Thus, mathematical symbols and words of literature are strata of an all-inclusive symbolical medium. Like Descartes' and Leibniz', Novalis' thought and effort was directed toward a universal medium of representation. These endeavors are revealed both in his philosophical fragments and in his strictly literary works.

7. MATHEMATICS AND MUSIC

> May not Music be described as the Mathematic of sense, Mathematic as the Music of the reason? The soul of each the same! Thus the musician *feels* Mathematic, the mathematician *thinks* Music, – Music the dream, Mathematic the working life – each to receive its consummation from the other when the human intelligence, elevated to its perfect type, shall shine forth glorified in some future Mozart-Dirichlet – or Beethoven-Gauss – a union already not indistinctly foreshadowed in the genius and labours of a Helmholtz! ("Trilogy," *Philos. Transact.*, CLIV (1864), Part III, p. 613).
>
> J. J. SYLVESTER, 1864

In Western civilization there is an ancient tradition of various associations of mathematics and music. Many great mathematicians felt impelled to treat music mathematically. Euclid is reported to have written a study on music which has not been preserved. Descartes wrote a *Compendium musicae* (1650). Kepler in his work *Harmonices mundi* (1619) perceives a subconscious mingling of music and mathematics in the human mind. Leibniz comments on this subconscious process as follows: "Die Musik ist eine verborgene arithmetische Übung der Seele, welche dabei nicht weiss, dass sie mit Zahlen umgeht. Die Seele vollbringt nämlich vieles in unklarer und unbemerkter Erkenntnistätigkeit, was sie mittels deutlicher Wahrnehmung nicht bemerken kann. Denn diejenigen sind im Irrtum, welche meinen, es könne nichts in der Seele geschehen, dessen sie selbst sich nicht bewusst werde. Wenn daher die Seele auch nicht merkt, dass sie rechnet, so fühlt sie doch die Wirkung dieser unbemerkten Rechnung, sei es als Freude am Zusammenklang oder als Bedrückung am Missklang" (as translated from the original Latin and quoted by Louis Locher-Ernst, "Mathematik und Musik," *Mathematik als Vorschule der Geist-Erkenntnis*, Zürich, 1944, p. 64). Euler wrote a mathematical treatise on music entitled *Tentamen novae theoriae musicae ex certissimis principiis dilucide expositae* (1739), in which he propounded his idea that musical intervals correspond to simple ratios of numbers (see Leonardi Eulera *Opera Omnia*, Lipsiae et Berolini, 1926, Series tertia, Volumen primum, P. xv). Novalis had among his books a copy of Chladni's *Entdeckung über die Theorie des Klanges* (Leipzig, 1787). In this book Chladni had recorded the results of his research on the vibrations of round and square plates, and of bells and rings. The French mathematician Joseph Fourier, another contemporary of Novalis, was able to demonstrate that all sounds, vocal or instrumental, are completely describable in mathematical terms. He represented sounds by sine and cosine functions whose graphs indicated loudness, pitch, and quality of a musical sound by the amplitude, frequency, and shape of the graph, respectively (see Kline, *op. cit.*, p. 287). After Novalis' time, the physicist and mathematician Helmholtz offered for the first time a physiological explanation of dissonance and other musical phenomena in his *Lehre von den Tonempfindungen als physiologische Grundlage für die Theorie der Musik* (1862). In our age, the late American mathematician George D. Birkhoff in his study *Aesthetic Measure* (Cambridge, Mass., 1933) and the Swiss mathematician Andreas Speiser in his work *Die mathematische Denkweise*, 3rd ed. (Basel, 1952) have seriously devoted themselves to the investigation of the interrelationships and analogies between music and mathematics.

One origin of this traditional association of music and mathematics is usually seen in the discovery of Pythagoras that the pitch of a sound from a plucked string depends on the length of the string and that harmonious sounds are given off by strings, the ratios of whose lengths are simple integers (Kline, p. 287). To the Pythagoreans, therefore, music was a manifestation of mathematical laws. They believed in the harmony of the spheres in the universe, *i.e.*, a musical harmony, dependent on mathematical number, hence also a mathematical harmony, the latter invisible, the former inaudible to the human organs of sense perception. The Pythagorean alliance of music, mathematics, and astronomy, re-emerged in the Middle Ages in the quadrivium of the curriculum in *artes liberales*: arithmetic, geometry, astronomy, and music.

Viewed against this long tradition of musical-mathematical relations, Novalis' fragments on music and mathematics no longer appear to be out of the ordinary. Moreover, most German Romanticists were preoccupied with music, although only Novalis devoted himself seriously to the more specific aspect of music in the Pythagorean and Chladnian sphere of meaning. The claim of Fritz Strich that "von allen Künsten liebte die Romantik jene am meisten, welche eine tönende Offenbarung der reinen Mathematik ist: die Musik" (*Deutsche Klassik und Romantik*, oder Vollendung und Unendlichkeit. Ein Vergleich, München, 1928, p. 250) is, in its mathematical implication, valid with regard to Novalis, and possibly Friedrich Schlegel and Kleist (see Silz, *op. cit.*, pp. 16, 135), but not with regard to the conception of music of all Romanticists.

The analogies between music and mathematics that have been pointed out at various times fall roughly into two categories: acoustical and structural. Andreas Speiser remarks in this connection: "In früheren Zeiten ist der arithmetische Charakter der Musik unbestritten gewesen, weil jedermann bei den Zahlen unmittelbar an Töne dachte. Heute denkt man unter dem Einfluss der analytischen Geometrie an räumliche, visuelle Dinge, nicht an akustische" (p. 23).

Novalis' fragments on music and mathematics reveal the timehonored themes linking these fields of endeavor. Leibniz' conception of music as a hidden arithmetic exercise of the human soul is reflected in the following of Novalis' fragments: "Unsere Seele weiss von Musik und hat daran Gefallen" (III, 158). "Das Gedächtnis treibt prophetischen – musikalischen Kalkül... Alle Erinnerung beruht auf indirektem Kalkül – auf Musik etc." (III, 251). The ancient Pythagorean idea of the harmony of the spheres is indistinctly yet recognizably manifested in another fragment: "Die musikalischen Verhältnisse scheinen mir recht eigentlich die Grundverhältnisse der Natur zu sein" (III, 291). "Musik als Bildnerin und Besänftigerin des Weltalls" (III, 117). The various themes on the relations of music and mathematics, with a reference to Pythagoras and Leibniz, are combined in the following fragment entitled *"Musik. Mathematik:"*

Hat die Musik nicht etwas von der kombinatorischen Analysis und umgekehrt? Zahlenharmonien – Zahlenakustik – gehört zur kombinatorischen Analysis.
 Die Zähler sind die mathematischen Vokale – alle Zahlen sind Zähler.
 Die kombinatorische Analysis führt auf das Zahlenphantasieren – und lehrt die Zahlenkompositionskunst – den mathematischen Generalbass. (Pythagoras, Leibniz). Die Sprache ist ein musikalisches Ideeninstrument. Der Dichter, Rhetor und Philosoph spielen und komponieren grammatisch. Eine Fuge ist durchaus logisch oder wissenschaftlich. – Sie kann auch poetisch behandelt werden. Der Generalbass enthält die musikalische Algeber und Analysis. Die kombinatorische Analysis ist die kritische Algeber und Analysis – und die musikalische Kompositionslehre verhält sich zum Generalbass wie die kombinatorische Analysis zur einfachen Analysis.
(III, 205f.).

In this fragment we perceive reverberations of Leibniz' *Ars combinatoria* and the combinatorial school of mathematics. Novalis manipulates kaleidoscopically music, grammar, and mathematics in the search for the best method of integrating them into his universal encyclopedia. He regards a fugue as a structure both logical and scientific. This view is shared by Speiser, who systematically explored the structural analogies of fugues and mathematical systems (see Speiser, pp. 23-36).

Finally, music and mathematics are enthusiastically fused by Novalis in his hymns to mathematics: "Echte Mathematik ist das eigentliche Element des Magiers. In der Musik erscheint sie förmlich als Offenbarung, als schaffender Idealism. Hier legitimiert sie sich als himmlische Gesandtin, kat' anthropon.... Aller Genuss ist musikalisch, mithin mathematisch" (III, 295f).

In the preceding section we already discussed the reflections of the associations of music and mathematics in *Die Lehrlinge zu Sais*.

For further discussion of the relation of Novalis to music see especially Karl Theodor Bluth, *Philosophische Probleme in den Aphorismen Hardenbergs* (Jena, 1914) and A. J. M. Bus, *Der Mythus der Musik in Novalis' Heinrich von Ofterdingen* (Alkmaar, 1947).

SUMMARY AND CONCLUSIONS

In his fragments on mathematics Novalis is concerned with an extension of this science beyond its usual domain and with its elucidation in broad contexts of art, life, and thought, and not with strict mathematical research. He regards mathematics as the ideal science and intends to use it as a unifying principle in his contemplated universal encyclopedia of knowledge. Besides the physical sciences, all other branches of knowledge are to be mathematized. Many of his fragments on mathematics, accordingly, deal with the mathematical features of various branches of knowledge and with the projection of mathematical concepts and symbols into these fields. In the spirit of irrational rationalism, many eighteenth century philosophers, and even mathematicians, linked mathematics with a number of non-physical branches of knowledge. The second half of the eighteenth century, and, in particular, the last decade, was not only a time of political upheavals (the French Revolution), of landmarks in philosophy (Kant's *Critiques*) and in German literature, but also of bold hypotheses and great discoveries in the natural sciences (oxygen, phenomena of electricity), and of lively fluctuations in the foundations of mathematics. Novalis took a vital interest in these developments. He was fascinated by discoveries that had turned alchemy into chemistry. If, in the spirit of mathematics, mere philosophical speculation on the nature of the universe had developed into physics, alchemy into chemistry, quackery into medicine, astrology into astronomy, and, more generally, speculative branches of knowledge into systematic sciences with logical structures and empirical bases, why should it not be possible to continue this process and mathematize religion, magic, music, or even poetry? In the process of mathematization, however, mathematics itself was to be broadened and deepened along the lines of Descartes' search for a "mathesis universalis" and Leibniz' search for an "arithmetica universalis." The universal arithmetic was to include all mental operations, volitional and aesthetic experiences, and all knowledge.

Both in the philosophical and novelistic fragments, as well as in his poetry, there is a vision of a future realm of final and absolute synthesis, a state of "coincidentia oppositorum," with mathematics elevated to a higher symbolism embracing language, music, magic, and religious rites, with man communicating in this symbolic language with nature, as in a fairy tale, with the laws of nature rescinded, and the law of contradiction repealed, a realm ruled by the poet-priest-musician-magician-mathematician.

Throughout his brief adult life of about ten years, Novalis was concerned with mathematics. In the earlier stages conventional mathematics predominated; in the later stages magical mathematics prevailed. At the University at Leipzig and the Mining Academy at Freiberg, and through continuous self-study, Novalis had acquired a thorough grounding in mathematics, grasping this subject both in its formal aspects and its philosophical implications. During Sophie's illness he clung to mathematics as to a firm prop. In intensity and continuity, Novalis' preoccupation with mathematics, and philosophy, is surpassed by no other intellectual pursuit of his. Evaluated in terms of his contributions, it is surpassed by his literary achievement. Judged by the effect of Novalis' works and thought on posterity, the fragments and strictly literary works are about equal.

Our image of Novalis needs to be modified. He was not an anemic aesthete, even after Sophie's death, immersed only in night and death, but rather a universal mind, embryonic, yet potentially of the order of Goethe. His activities and pursuits embraced the whole range designated by the extremes, no extremes to Novalis at that, of religious fervor and earthly sensuality, of music and engineering, of night and day, of death and life, of poetry and mathematics.

BIBLIOGRAPHY

Note. This bibliography is limited to studies elucidating some aspect of the relation of Novalis to mathematics. Asterisks denote items, mostly unpublished dissertations, inaccessible to the author.

1. EDITIONS OF NOVALIS WORKS

Schriften, ed. F. Schlegel & L. Tieck. 2 vols. Berlin, 1802.
Schriften, ed. L. Tieck & E. v. Bülow, 6th ed., Berlin, 1846.
Schriften, ed. Carl Meissner. 3 vols. Leipzig, 1898.
Werke, ed. J. Dohmke. Leipzig, 1892.
Schriften, ed. E. Heilborn. 3 vols. Berlin, 1901.
Schriften, ed. J. Minor. 4 vols. Jena, 1907.
Werke, ed. H. Friedmann. 3 vols. Berlin, 1913.
Sämtliche Werke, ed. E. Kamnitzer. 4 vols. Munich, 1924.
Fragmente, ed. E. Kamnitzer. Dresden, 1929.
Schriften, ed. P. Kluckhohn & R. Samuel. 4 vols. Leipzig, 1929.
Briefe und Werke, ed. E. Wasmuth. 3 vols. Berlin, 1943.
Werke, Briefe, Dokumente, ed. E. Wasmuth. 4 vols. Heidelberg, 1954-1957.
Gesammelte Werke, ed. C. Seelig. 5 vols. Herrliberg-Zürich, 1945-1946.

2. STUDIES ON NOVALIS

ALBRECHT, LUITGARD. *Der magische Idealismus in Novalis' Märchentheorie und Märchendichtung*. Hamburg, 1948.
ALLEMANN, BEDA. *Ironie und Dichtung*. Pfullingen, 1956.
ANRICH, ELSMARIE. *Grossgöttliche Ordnung: Thomas von Aquin, Paracelsus, Novalis und die Astrologie*. Tübingen, 1951.
AUGENSTEIN, A. H. VON. "Zur Textgeschichte von Novalis' Fragmenten," *Euphorion*, XIII (1906).
BENZ, RICHARD. *Die Welt der Dichter und der Musik*, 2nd. ed. Düsseldorf, 1949.
BESSER, KURT. *Die Problematik der aphoristischen Form bei Lichtenberg, Schlegel, Novalis und Nietzsche*. Berlin, 1935.
BESSET, MAURICE. *Novalis et la pensée mystique*. Paris, 1947.
*BETZ, ERNST. *Die Dichtungen des Novalis; ihr Kompositionsprinzip; der Ausdruck seiner Geschichtsauffassung*. Diss. Erlangen, 1954.
BISER, EUGEN. *Abstieg und Aufstieg; die geistige Welt in Novalis' "Hymnen an die Nacht."* Heidelberg, 1954.
BLUTH, KARL THEODOR. *Philosophische Probleme in den Aphorismen Hardenbergs*. Diss. Jena, 1914.
BLUTH, KARL THEODOR. *Medizingeschichtliches bei Novalis*. Berlin, 1934.
BOLLINGER, HEINZ. *Die Lehrlinge zu Sais; Versuch einer Erläuterung*. Winthertur, 1954.
BOLLNOW, OTTO FRIEDRICH. "Zum Weg nach innen bei Novalis," *Unruhe und Geborgenheit im Weltbild neuerer Dichter*, 2nd ed. Stuttgart, 1958.
BONARIUS, GERHARD. *Zum magischen Idealismus bei Keats und Novalis*. Giessen, 1950.
*BORST, OTTO. *Friedrich von Hardenbergs Wirkungen in der zweiten und dritten Phase der deutschen Romantik*. Diss. Tübingen, 1956.
BUS, A. J. M. *Der Mythus der Musik in "Heinrich von Ofterdingen."* Diss. Amsterdam, 1947.

BUSSE, CARL. *Novalis' Lyrik*. Oppeln, 1898.
*BRUNSBACH, WILFRIED. *Erlebnis und Gestaltung der Natur bei Friedrich von Hardenberg/Novalis: eine Studie zur Phänomenologie der Frühromantik*. Diss. Bonn, 1951.
CALVEZ, JEAN-YVES. "Novalis et la philosophie," *Études Germaniques*, XII (1957).
CARLSSON, ANNI. *Die Fragmente des Novalis*. Basel, 1939.
CARLYLE, THOMAS. "Novalis," *Critical and Miscellaneous Essays*. London, 1845.
*CREMERS, P. J. *Der magische Idealismus als dichterisches Formproblem in den Werken Friedrich von Hardenbergs*. Diss. Bonn, 1921.
DIEZ, MAX. "Metapher und Märchengestalt III: Novalis und das allegorische Märchen," *PMLA*, XLVIII (1933).
DILTHEY, WILHELM. "Novalis," *Das Erlebnis und die Dichtung*, 10th ed. Leipzig & Berlin, 1929. First book ed., 1905. Article first appeared in *Preussische Jahrbücher*, 1865.
DYCK, MARTIN. *The Relation of Novalis to Mathematics*. Diss. Cincinnati, 1956.
DYCK, MARTIN. "Theodor Haering: *Novalis als Philosoph* (review article)", *Comparative Literature*, VIII (1956).
EDERHEIMER, EDGAR. *Jakob Böhme und die Romantiker*. Heidelberg, 1904.
EMGE, C. A. "Das Unendliche bei Novalis," *Archiv für Rechts- und Wirtschaftsphilosophie*, XVII (1923-1924).
FAUTECK, H. *Die Sprachtheorie Friedrich von Hardenbergs*. Berlin, 1940.
*FLICKENSCHILD, URSULA. *Novalis' Begegnung mit Fichte und Hemsterhuis*. Diss. Kiel, 1947.
FLÖRCKE, W. *Novalis und die Musik mit besonderer Berücksichtigung des Musikalischen in Novalis' "Hymnen an die Nacht."* Diss. Marburg, 1928.
FRANK, E. *Friedrich von Hardenbergs philosophische Anschauungen*. Diss. Köln, 1921.
FRIEDELL, EGON. *Novalis als Philosoph*. München, 1904.
GREINER, MARTIN. *Das frühromantische Naturgefühl in der Lyrik von Tieck und Novalis*. Leipzig, 1930.
*GRIESSMANN, HELMUT. *Die Raumgestaltung in Friedrich von Hardenbergs "Heinrich von Ofterdingen" und Otto Ludwigs "Zwischen Himmel und Erde."* Diss. Bonn, 1955.
GOLDAMMER, KURT. *Novalis und die Welt des Ostens*. Stuttgart, 1948.
HAERING, THEODOR. *Novalis als Philosoph*. Stuttgart, 1954.
HAMBURGER, KÄTE. "Novalis und die Mathematik; eine Studie zur Erkenntnistheorie der Romantik," *Romantik-Forschungen*. Deutsche Vierteljahrsschrift für Literaturwissenschaft und Geistesgeschichte, Buchreihe, Vol. 16. Halle, 1929.
HAMBURGER, MICHAEL. *Reason and Energy: Studies in German Literature*. London, 1957.
HAUSSMANN, J. F. "German Estimates of Novalis from 1800 to 1850," *Modern Philology*, IX (1911-1912).
HAUSSMANN, J. F. "Die deutsche Kritik über Novalis von 1850-1900," *The Journal of English and Germanic Philology*, XI (1913).
HAVENSTEIN, EDUARD. *Friedrich von Hardenbergs ästhetische Anschauungen*. Palaestra, LXXXIV. Berlin, 1909.
HAYWOOD, BRUCE. *A Study of Imagery in the Works of Novalis*. Diss. Harvard, 1956.
HEDERER, EDGAR. *Novalis*. Wien, 1949.
*HELLMER, ELISABETH. *Friedrich Schlegel und Novalis nach ihren Briefen*. Diss. München, 1954.
HEILBORN, ERNST. *Novalis, der Romantiker*. Berlin, 1901.
HENSEL, PAUL. *Novalis' magischer Idealismus*. Tübingen, 1930.

HERZOG, WERNER. *Mystik und Lyrik bei Novalis.* Stuttgart, 1928.
HIEBEL, FRIEDRICH. *Novalis, der Dichter der blauen Blume.* Bern, 1951.
HIEBEL, FRIEDRICH. *Novalis; German Poet, European Thinker, Christian Mystic.* University of North Carolina Studies in Germanic Languages and Literatures, No. 10. Chapel Hill, 1954.
HIEBEL, FRIEDRICH. "Novalis and the Problem of Romanticism," *Monatshefte,* XXXIX (1947).
HIEBEL, FRIEDRICH. "Goethe's "Märchen" in the Light of Novalis," *PMLA,* LXIII (1948).
HIPPEL, ERNST VON. "Novalis und Hemsterhuis," *Künder der Humanität.* Bonn, 1946.
HOFMANN, KARL. "Der Dichter Novalis in Freiberg," *Mitteilungen des Freiberger Altertumsvereins,* Heft 57. Freiberg, 1927.
HÖFT, ALBERT. *Novalis als Künstler des Fragments.* Diss. Göttingen, 1935.
IMLE, FANNY. *Novalis; seine philosophische Weltanschauung.* Paderborn, 1928.
IBEL, RUDOLF. *Weltanschauung deutscher Dichter.* Hamburg, 1948.
JAEGER, HANS PETER. *Hölderlin-Novalis. Grenzen der Sprache.* Zürich, 1949.
KAMLA, HENRY. *Novalis' "Hymnen an die Nacht."* Kopenhagen, 1945.
*KIRCHNER, WILHELM. *Die persönliche Stileinheit der Weltanschauung des Novalis.* Diss. Würzburg, 1949.
KLEEBERG, LUDWIG. "Novalis und Eckartshausen," *Euphorion,* XXII (1920).
KLEEBERG, LUDWIG. "Studien zu Novalis," *Euphorion,* XXIII (1921).
KLUCKHOHN, PAUL. *Schillers Wirkungen auf Friedrich von Hardenberg.* Stuttgart, 1934.
KOHLSCHMIDT, WERNER. "Der Wortschatz der Innerlichkeit bei Novalis," *Festschrift für H. Schneider und P. Kluckhohn,* Tübingen, 1948.
KOMMERELL, MAX. "Novalis Hymnen an die Nacht," *Gedicht und Gedanke,* ed. H. O. Burger, Halle 1942.
KUHN, HUGO. "Poetische Synthesis oder Ein kritischer Versuch über romantische Philosophie und Poesie aus Novalis' Fragmenten," *Zeitschrift für philosophische Forschung,* V (1951).
*KÜPPER, PETER. *Untersuchung zum Zeitmotiv und Zeitproblem im Werke des Novalis.* Diss. Köln, 1954.
KUEHNLE, KARL. "Das Weltgefühl bei Novalis," *Geistige Welt,* II (1947-1948).
LANGHAMMER, FRANZ. *Das Novalisbild im Frankreich des neunzehnten Jahrhunderts.* Diss. Northwestern, 1956.
LEWIS, LETA JANE. *Friedrich von Hardenberg (Novalis) in the Light of East Indian Philosophy and Religion.* Diss. California, Los Angeles, 1958.
LICHTENBERGER, HENRI, *Novalis.* Paris, 1912.
*LUTHER, BEATE. *Bedeutungsbereiche bei Novalis. Dargestellt am Traum von der blauen Blume.* Diss. München, 1955.
LÜTZELER, HEINRICH. "Novalis und Hemsterhuis," *Neue Jahrbücher für Wissenschaft,* I (1925).
MATENKO, PERCY. "Fragments from Longfellow's Workshop: Novalis," *Germanic Review,* XXII (1947).
MAY, KURT. "Weltbild und innere Form der Klassik und Romantik in Wilhelm Meister und Heinrich von Ofterdingen," *Romantik-Forschungen,* Halle, 1929.
MEYER, RUDOLF. *Novalis, Das Christuserlebnis und die neue Geistesoffenbarung.* Stuttgart, 1939, 2nd ed., 1954.
*MINNIGERODE, IRMTRUD VON. *Die Christusanschauung des Novalis.* Diss. Tübingen, 1941.
MÜLLER, PAUL EMANUEL. *Novalis' Märchenwelt.* Diss. Zürich, 1953.
MÜLLER-SEIDEL, WALTER. "Probleme neuerer Novalisforschung," *Germanisch-Romanische Monatsschrift,* XXXIV (1953).

NIVELLE, ARMAND. "Die Auffassung der Poesie in den Fragmenten von Novalis," *Tijdschrift voor levende talen*, XV (1949).
OBENAUER, KARL JUSTUS. *Hölderlin - Novalis*. Jena, 1925.
OLSHAUSEN, WALDEMAR. *Friedrich von Hardenbergs (Novalis) Beziehungen zur Naturwissenschaft seiner Zeit*. Diss. Leipzig, 1905.
OVERBECK, HELENE. *Die religiöse Weltanschauung des Novalis*. Diss. Berlin, 1928.
PIXBERG, HERMANN. *Novalis als Naturphilosoph*. Gütersloh, 1928.
REBLE, ALBERT. "Märchen und Wirklichkeit bei Novalis," *Deutsche Vierteljahrsschrift für Literaturwissenschaft und Geistesgeschichte*, XIX (1941).
REED, EUGENE E. "Novalis 'Heinrich von Ofterdingen' as 'Gesamtkunstwerk'," *Philological Quarterly*, XXXIII (1954).
REHM, WALTER. *Orpheus. Der Dichter und die Toten. Selbstdeutung und Totenkult bei Novalis - Hölderlin - Rilke*. Düsseldorf, 1950.
RITTER, HEINZ. *Novalis' Hymnen an die Nacht*. Heidelberg, 1930.
ROOS, JAQUES. *Aspects littéraires du mysticisme philosophique et l'influence de Boehme et de Swedenborg au debut du romantisme: W. Blake, Novalis, Ballanche*. Strassbourg, 1951.
SAMUEL, RICHARD, editor. *Novalis. Der handschriftliche Nachlass. Versteigerungskatalog*. Berlin, 1930.
SAMUEL, RICHARD. "Der berufliche Werdegang Friedrich von Hardenbergs," *Romantik-Forschungen*. Halle, 1929.
SAMUEL, RICHARD. "Zur Geschichte des Nachlasses Friedrich von Hardenbergs (Novalis)," *Jahrbuch der deutschen Schillergesellschaft*, II (1958).
*SCHMID, HEINZ DIETER. *Friedrich von Hardenberg (Novalis) und Abraham Gottlob Werner*. Diss. Tübingen, 1952.
*SCHMIDT, RUDOLF WOLFGANG. *Die Endzeitvorstellungen bei Novalis. Studien zum Problem der Eschatologie in der deutschen Romantik*. Diss. Wien, 1956.
SCHRIMPF, HANS JOACHIM. "Novalis' Lied der Toten," *Die deutsche Lyrik*, ed. B. v. Wiese, Vol. I. Düsseldorf, 1956.
*SCHULZ, GERHARD. *Die Berufstätigkeit Friedrich von Hardenbergs (Novalis) und ihre Bedeutung für seine Dichtung und seine Gedankenwelt*. Diss. Leipzig, 1958.
SIMON, HEINRICH. *Der magische Idealismus. Studien zur Philosophie des Novalis*. Heidelberg, 1906.
SPRING, POWELL. *Novalis, Pioneer of the Spirit*. Winterpark, Florida, 1946.
SPENLÉ, E. *Novalis, essai sur l'idéalisme romantique en Allemagne*. Paris, 1904.
STANGE, CARL. "Novalis' Weltanschauung," *Zeitschrift für systematische Theologie*, I (1922).
STEINER, RUDOLF. *Novalis als Verkünder des spirituell zu erfassenden Christentums*. Dornach, 1930.
*STRIEDTER, JURY. *Die Fragmente des Novalis als 'Praefigurationen' seiner Dichtung*. Diss. Heidelberg, 1953.
TERZAGA, A. "Novalis y la poesia absoluta," *Sur* (Buenos Aires), Jan.-Feb., 1952.
*TSCHENG-DSCHE-FENG, *Die Analogie von Natur und Geist als Stilprinzip in Novalis' Dichtung*. Diss. Heidelberg, 1935.
TOURNOUX, G. A. *La langue de Novalis*. Paris, 1920.
*TROSIENER, IRMGARD. *Der Wechselbezug von Einzelnem und Ganzem in den Fragmenten des Novalis*. Diss. Freiburg i. Br., 1955.
WAGNER, LYDIA ELISABETH. *The Scientific Interest of Friedrich von Hardenberg (Novalis)*. Ann Arbor, 1937.
WALZEL, OSKAR. "Die Formkunst von Novalis' 'Heinrich von Ofterdingen'," *Germanisch-Romanische Monatsschrift*, VII (1919).
WASMUTH, EWALD. "Novalis' Beitrag zu einer 'Physik in einem höheren Sinne'," *Neue Schweizer Rundschau*, Neue Folge, XVIII (1950-1951).

WEIHE, A. *Der junge Eichendorff und Novalis' Naturpantheismus.* Berlin, 1939.
*WEYMANN, ALBRECHT. *Novalis' Gedanken zur Psychologie.* Diss. Berlin, 1929.
ZIEGLER, KLAUS. "Die Religiosität des Novalis im Spiegel der Hymnen an die Nacht," *Zeitschrift für deutsche Philologie,* LXX (1947-1949), LXXI (1953).

3. STUDIES ON GERMAN ROMANTICISM, MATHEMATICS, AND PHILOSOPHY

ADICKES, ERICH. *Kant als Naturforscher.* 2 vols. Berlin, 1924.
Acta Eruditorum. Leipzig, 1682-1782.
AHRENS, WILHELM. *Scherz und Ernst in der Mathematik. Geflügelte und ungeflügelte Worte.* Leipzig, 1904.
ALLEMAN, BEDA. "Der frühromantische Begriff einer modernen Literaturwissenschaft," *Über das Dichterische.* Pfullingen, 1957.
Allgemeine Deutsche Biographie. 56 vols. Leipzig, 1875-1912.
APOSTLE, HIPPOCRATES G. *Aristotle's Philosophy of Mathematics.* Chicago, 1952.
*ARNOLD, GEORG. *Sacra mathesis.* Altorf, 1676.
Athenaeum, ed. A. W. & F. Schlegel. 3 vols. Berlin, 1798-1800.
BAADER, FRANZ XAVER VON. *Sämtliche Werke.* 14 vols. Leipzig, 1852-1857.
BAUMGART, DAVID. *Franz von Baader und die philosophische Romantik.* Halle, 1927.
BECKER, OSKAR. *Mathematische Existenz.* Halle, 1927.
BECKER, OSKAR, and JOSEPH EHRENFRIED HOFMANN. *Geschichte der Mathematik.* Bonn, 1951.
BELL, ERIC T. *Men of Mathematics.* New York, 1937.
BELL, ERIC T. *Mathematics, Queen and Servant of Science.* New York, 1951.
BENSE, MAX. *Konturen einer Geistesgeschichte der Mathematik.* 2 vols. Hamburg, 1948, 1949.
BENTLEY, A. F. *A Linguistic Analysis of Mathematics.* Bloomington, 1932.
BENZ, RICHARD. *Die deutsche Romantik,* 5th ed. Stuttgart, 1956. First ed., 1937.
BENZ, RICHARD. *Lebenswelt der Romantik. Dokumente romantischen Denkens und Seins.* Munich, 1948.
BENZ, RICHARD. *Die Zeit der deutschen Klassik.* Stuttgart, 1953.
BIETAK, WILHELM. *Romantische Wissenschaft.* Leipzig, 1940.
BINGEL, H. A. G. *Werner und die Theorie der Gebirgsbildung.* Diss. Marburg, 1933.
BINDEL, ERNST. *Die Zahlengrundlagen der Musik im Wandel der Zeiten.* 2 vols. Stuttgart, 1950, 1951.
BIRKHOFF, GEORGE. *Aesthetic Measure.* Cambridge, Mass., 1933.
BLASCHKE, WILHELM. *Mathematik und Leben.* Wiesbaden, 1950.
BLOOMFIELD, LEONARD. "Linguistic Aspects of Science," *International Encyclopedia of Unified Science.* Vol. I, No. 4. Chicago, 1939.
BOYER, CARL B. *The Concepts of Calculus.* New York, 1949.
BORDEN, FRIEDRICH. "Die deutsche Romantik und die Wissenschaft, eine Untersuchung über den romantischen Wissenschaftsbegriff," *Archiv für Kulturgeschichte,* XXI (1930).
BRUMBAUGH, ROBERT S. *Plato's Mathematical Imagination.* Bloomington, 1954.
BULLE, F. *Hemsterhuis und der Irrationalismus des 18. Jahrh.* Diss. Jena, 1911.
BURJA, ABEL. *Der selbstlernende Algebraist, oder Anweisung zur ganzen Rechenkunst.* 2 vols. Berlin, 1786.

99

BÜSCH, JOHANN GEORG. *Versuch einer Mathematik zum Nutzen und Vergnügen des bürgerlichen Lebens.* 4th ed., Hamburg, 1798. First ed., 1773.
BUTTE, WILHELM. *Grundlinien einer Arithmetik des menschlichen Lebens.* Landshut, 1811.
CAJORI, FLORIAN. *A History of Mathematics*, 2nd ed. New York, 1929.
CANTOR, MORITZ. *Vorlesungen über Geschichte der Mathematik.* 4 vols. Leipzig, 1880-1908.
CARLYLE, THOMAS. *Critical and Miscellaneous Essays.* London, 1845.
CASSIRER, ERNST. "Kant und die moderne Mathematik," *Kantstudien,* XII (1907).
CASSIRER, ERNST. *Philosophie der symbolischen Formen.* 3 vols. Berlin, 1923, 1925, 1929.
CASSIRER, ERNST. *Substanzbegriff und Fuuktionsbegriff,* 2nd ed. Berlin, 1923.
CHLADNI, ERNST FLORENS FRIEDRICH. *Entdeckung über die Theorie des Klanges.* Leipzig, 1787.
DUBISLAV, W. *Die Definition.* Leipzig, 1931.
DYCK, MARTIN. *Goethe und die Mathematik.* M. A. Thesis, Manitoba, 1954.
DYCK, MARTIN. "Goethe's Views on Pure Mathematics," *Germanic Review,* XXXI (1956).
DYCK, MARTIN. "Goethe's Thought in the Light of his Pronouncements on Applied and Misapplied Mathematics," *PMLA,* LXXIII (1958).
EISENHART, L. P. *Coordinate Geometry.* Boston, 1939.
EUCLID, *Elements. Great Books of the Western World,* XI. Chicago, 1952.
EULER, LEONHARD. *Institutiones calculi differentialis.* St. Petersburg, 1755.
EULER, LEONHARD. *Differenzial-Rechnung,* transl. by J. A. C. Michelsen. Berlin, 1790-1793.
EULER, LEONHARD. *Vollständige Anleitung zur Algebra.* St. Petersburg, 1770.
EULER, LEONHARD. *Leonardi Eulera Opera Omnia.* Lipsiae et Berolini, 1908 ff.
FICHTE, JOHANN GOTTLIEB. *Werke,* ed. F. Medicus. 6 vols. Leipzig, 1922.
FINK, A. H. *Maxime und Fragment.* München, 1934.
FISCHER, ERNST GOTTFRIED. *Theorie der Dimensionszeichen.* Berlin, 1791.
FISCHER, LUDWIG. *Die Grundlagen der Philosophie und Mathematik.* Leipzig, 1933.
GATZ, FELIX M. *Musik-Ästhetik in ihren Hauptrichtungen.* Stuttgart, 1929.
GODE- VON AESCH, ALEXANDER. *Natural Science in German Romanticism.* New York, 1941.
GRASSL, ANTON. *Die Romantik, ein Gegenpol der Technik.* Bonn, 1954.
HANS, WILHELM. "Kant und die Romantik," *Euphorion,* XIII (1906).
HARTMANN, NIKOLAI. *Die Philosophie des deutschen Idealismus.* 2 vols. Berlin & Leipzig, 1923.
HAYM, RUDOLF. *Die romantische Schule,* 4th ed. Berlin, 1920. First ed., 1870.
HELMHOLTZ, H. L. F. VON. *Lehre von den Tonempfindungen als physiologische Grundlage für die Theorie der Musik.* 1862.
HEMSTERHUIS, FRANZ. *Oeuvres philosophiques.* 2 vols. Paris, 1809.
HETTNER, HERMANN. *Die romantische Schule in ihrem Zusammenhange mit Goethe und Schiller.* Braunschweig, 1850.
HILBERT, DAVID. "Die logischen Grundlagen der Mathematik," *Mathematische Annalen,* LXXXVIII (1922).
HILBERT, DAVID. "Über das Unendliche," *Mathematische Annalen,* XCV (1925).
HILBERT, DAVID. *Grundlagen der Geometrie,* 7th ed. Leipzig & Berlin, 1930.
HILBERT, DAVID, and W. ACKERMANN. *Grundzüge der theoretischen Logik,* 2nd ed. Berlin, 1938.
HINDENBURG, KARL FRIEDRICH. *Novi systematis permutationum, combinationum etc., primae liniae.* Leipzig, 1781.

HINDENBURG, KARL FRIEDRICH. *Der polynomische Lehrsatz.* Leipzig, 1796.
HINDENBURG, KARL FRIEDRICH. *Beschreibung einer ganz neuen Art, nach einem bekannten Gesetze fortgehende Zahlen durch Abzählen oder Abmessen bequem und sicher zu finden.* Leipzig, 1776.
HOFMANN, JOSEPH EHRENFRIED. *Die Entwicklungsgeschichte der Leibnizschen Mathematik.* Munich, 1949.
HOFMANN, JOSEPH EHRENFRIED. *Geschichte der Mathematik.* 3 vols. Berlin, 1953-1957.
HÖLDER, OTTO. *Die mathematische Methode.* Berlin, 1924.
HUCH, RICARDA. *Die Romantik.* 2 vols. Leipzig, 1899.
Journal de l'École polytechnique. Paris, 1794 ff.
Journal für die reine und angewandte Mathematik. Berlin & Leipzig, 1826 ff.
KANT, IMMANUEL. *Sämtliche Werke*, 12th ed. Leipzig, 1922.
KÄSTNER, ABRAHAM GOTTHELF. *Anfangsgründe der Analysis des Unendlichen*, 3rd ed. Göttingen, 1799. First ed., 1760.
KATTSOFF, LOUIS O. *A Philosophy of Mathematics.* Ames, 1948.
KÉRÉKJÁRTÓ, B. V. *Vorlesungen über Topologie.* Berlin, 1923.
KEYSER, CASSIUS J. *Mathematics as a Culture Clue.* New York, 1947.
KLEIN, FELIX. *Vorlesungen über die Entwicklung der Mathematik im neunzehnten Jahrhundert.* Berlin, 1926.
KLINE, MORRIS. *Mathematics in Western Culture.* New York, 1953.
KLUCKHOHN, PAUL. *Das Ideengut der deutschen Romantik*, 3rd ed. Tübingen, 1953.
KLUCKHOHN, PAUL. *Die deutsche Romantik.* Bielefeld & Leipzig, 1924.
KLUCKHOHN, PAUL, editor. *Weltanschauung der Frühromantik.* Leipzig, 1932.
KORFF, HERMANN AUGUST. *Geist der Goethezeit.* 4 vols. Leipzig, 1923-1953.
Die königlich sächsische Bergakademie. Freiberg, 1904.
LAGRANGE, JOSEPH LOUIS. *Théorie des fonctions analytiques*, 2nd ed. Paris, 1813. First ed., 1789.
LAGRANGE, JOSEPH LOUIS. *Theorie der analytischen Funktionen*, transl. Gruson. 2 vols. Berlin, 1798.
LAPLACE, PIERRE SIMON DE. *Exposition du système du monde*, 6th ed. Paris, 1878. First ed., 1796.
LAPLACE, PIERRE SIMON DE. *Darstellung des Weltsystems*, transl. J. K. F. Hauff. 2 vols. Frankfurt, 1797-1798.
LEIBNIZ, GOTTFRIED WILHELM. *Ars combinatoria.* 1668.
Leipziger Magazin für reine und angewandte Mathematik. Leipzig, 1786-1789.
LOCHER-ERNST, LOUIS. *Mathematik als Vorschule der Geist-Erkenntnis.* Zürich, 1944.
LOREY, WILHELM. "August Crelle zum Gedächtnis," *Journal für die reine und angewandte Mathematik,* CLVII (1926).
LOREY, WILHELM. "Goethes Stellung zur Mathematik," *Goethe als Seher und Erforscher der Natur*, ed. J. Walther. Weimar, 1930.
LOREY, WILHELM. *Das Studium der Mathematik an den deutschen Universitäten seit Anfang des neunzehnten Jahrhunderts.* Leipzig & Berlin, 1916.
MAHNKE, DIETRICH. *Unendliche Sphäre und Allmittelpunkt. Beiträge zur Genealogie der mathematischen Mystik.* Halle, 1937.
MALFATTI, GIOVANNI. *Studien über Anarchie und Hierarchie des Wissens.* Leipzig, 1845.
MAZIARZ, E. A. *The Philosophy of Mathematics.* New York, 1950.
MEHLIS, GEORG. *Die deutsche Romantik.* München, 1922.
MERRIMAN, GAYLORD M. *To Discover Mathematics.* New York, 1942.
MOOS, PAUL. *Die Philosophie der Musik.* Stuttgart, 1922.
MONTUCLA, J. F. *Histoire des Mathématiques*, 2nd ed. 4 vols. Paris, 1799. First ed., 1754.

MÜLLER, ADAM. *Vorlesungen über die deutsche Wissenschaft und Literatur.* 1806.
MÜLLER, ANDREAS, editor. *Kunstanschauung der Frühromantik.* Leipzig, 1931.
MÜLLER, MAX, translator. *Kant's Critique of Pure Reason.* London, 1905.
NATORP, PAUL. *Die logischen Grundlagen der exakten Naturwissenschaften.* Leipzig & Berlin, 1923.
PASCAL, BLAISE. *Pensée sur la religion et sur quelques autres sujets,* ed. A. Gazier. Paris, 1907.
PAULSEN, FRIEDRICH. *Geschichte des gelehrten Unterrichts auf den deutschen Schulen und Universitäten.* Leipzig, 1885.
PETERSEN, JULIUS. *Die Wesensbestimmung der deutschen Romantik.* Leipzig, 1926.
POINCARÉ, HENRI. *Wissenschaft und Hypothese,* transl. F. and L. Lindemann. Leipzig & Berlin, 1928.
PORTNOY, JULIUS. *The Philosopher and Music.* New York, 1954.
*PITCAIRN, ARCHIBALD. *Elementa medicinae physico-mathematica.* London, 1717.
RAND, BENJAMIN, editor. *Modern Classical Philosophers,* 2nd ed. Boston, 1936.
REHBEIN, J. H. E. *Versuch einer neuen Grundlegung der Geometrie.* Göttingen, 1795.
REHDER, HELMUT. *Die Philosophie der unendlichen Landschaft.* Halle, 1932.
REIFF, R. *Geschichte der unendlichen Reihen.* Tübingen, 1889.
ROSENBLOOM, PAUL. *The Elements of Mathematical Logic.* New York, 1950.
RUPRECHT, ERICH. *Der Aufbruch der romantischen Bewegung.* Munich, 1948.
SCHELLING, FRIEDRICH W. J. VON. *Von der Weltseele.* Hamburg, 1798.
SCHLEGEL, FRIEDRICH. *Literary Notebooks* 1797-1801, ed. Hans Eichner. London & Toronto, 1957.
SCHULZ, FRANZ. *Klassik und Romantik der Deutschen,* 2nd ed. Stuttgart, 1952.
SCHMID, J. J. *Biblischer mathematicus seu illustratio sacrae scripturae ex mathematicis scientiis.* 1736.
SILZ, WALTER. *Early German Romanticism.* Cambridge, Mass., 1929.
SMITH, D. E. *The Poetry of Mathematics.* New York, 1934.
SMITH, D. E. *A Source Book in Mathematics.* New York, 1929.
SMITH, N. K. *A Commentary to Kant's 'Critique of Pure Reason',* 2nd ed. London, 1932.
SPEISER, ANDREAS. *Die mathematische Denkweise.* Zürich, 1932.
SPEISER, ANDREAS. *Elemente der Philosophie und Mathematik.* Basel, 1952.
SPEISER, ANDREAS. *Die geistige Arbeit.* Basel & Stuttgart, 1955.
SPIESS, OTTO. *Leonhard Euler, ein Beitrag zur Geistesgeschichte des achtzehnten Jahrhunderts.* Frauenfeld & Leipzig, 1929.
STAHL, KONRAD DIETRICH MARTIN. *Anfangsgründe der Zahlenarithmetik und Buchstabenrechnung.* Jena, 1797.
STEINBÜCHEL, THEODOR. *Romantik: ein Zyklus Tübinger Vorlesungen.* Tübingen, 1948.
STEIN, ROBERT. "Naturwissenschaftliche Romantiker," *Archiv für Geschichte der Medizin,* XV (1923).
STRICH, FRITZ. *Deutsche Klassik und Romantik, oder Vollendung und Unendlichkeit. Ein Vergleich,* 2nd ed. Munich, 1928.
STRUIK, DIRK J. *A Concise History of Mathematics.* 2 vols. New York, 1948.
STURM, L. C. *Mathesis ad sacrae scripturae interpretationem applicata.* 1710.
SPINOZA, BENEDICT DE. *Ethica ordine geometrico demonstrata.* Amsterdam, 1677.
TIMERDING, H. E. *Die Verbreitung mathematischen Wissens und mathematischer Auffassung.* Berlin & Leipzig, 1914.
TÖPFER, HEINRICH AUGUST. *Kombinatorische Analytik.* Leipzig, 1793.

TROPFKE, JOHANNES. *Geschichte der Elementar-Mathematik*. 4 vols. Berlin & Leipzig, 1930.
ULLMANN, RICHARD, and HELENE GOTTHARD. *Geschichte des Begriffs Romantisch in Deutschland*. Berlin, 1927.
VOSS, A. *Über die mathematische Erkenntnis*. Leipzig & Berlin, 1914.
VOSS, A. *Die Beziehungen der Mathematik zur Kultur der Gegenwart*. Leipzig & Berlin, 1914.
VEGA, GEORG V. *Logarithmisch-trigonometrische Tafeln*, 2nd ed. Leipzig, 1800. First ed., 1793.
WALZEL, OSKAR. *Deutsche Romantik*, 5th ed. Leipzig & Berlin, 1923.
WILLOUGHBY, L. A. *The German Romantic Movement*. London, etc., 1930.
ZEYDEL, EDWIN H. *Ludwig Tieck, the German Romanticist*. Princeton & Cincinnati, 1935.
ZEYDEL, EDWIN H. *On Romanticism and the Art of Translation. Studies in Honor of Edwin Hermann Zeydel*, ed. G. F. Merkel. Princeton & Cincinnati, 1956.

INDEX

Academy of Science, at Berlin, 20, 24, 31, 47; St. Petersburg, 20.
acoustics & math., 58, 77, 92.
Acta Eruditorum, 20.
Adickes, E., 38.
aesthetics & math., preface, 62, 76, 90.
Ahrens, W., 87.
algebra, 7, 8, 12, 24, 26, 30, 35, 43, 46, 50, 52, *61-68*, 73, 78, 88.
analysis, *see* calculus, differential and integral; *see* synthesis.
aphorism, 1.
applicability of math., 77.
Aristotle, 78.
arithmetic, 7, 26, 38, 43, 46, *61-68*, 71, 73, 82, 91; dynamic a., 45; *see also specific concepts*.
"arithmetica universalis," 4, 12, 22, 29, 34, 44, 46, 61, 62, 87, 88, 93.
Arnold, G., 24.
"ars combinatoria," 28, 40, 65, 67, 92.
"ars inveniendi," 28, 40, 69, 73; *see also* free creation.
art, 40, 67.
astrology *or* astronomy, 6, 26, 34, 91, 93.
axiom *or* postulate, 7, 16, 32, 33, 44, 52, *55-57*.
Aubisson de Voisins, J. F., 36, 37.

Baader, F. von, 35, 38, 44, 45.
Baumgart, D. 45.
Becker, O., 38.
Beethoven, L. van, 89.
Berkeley, G., 50.
Bernoulli, Jacob, 20, 23, 47; Johann, 20, 21, 23.

Besset, M., 18, 19, 61.
Bezont, E., 50.
Bietak, W., 25.
binary system of notation, 23.
Birkhoff, G. D., 90.
Bluth, K. Th., 13, 92.
body, 16, 59; b. & soul, 80.
Böhme, J., 2, 33, 38.
Bollinger, H., 88.
Bolyai, F., 55.
botany, 59.
Boyer, C., 20, 49.
Buffon, G. L. L., compte de, 24.
Bülow, E. von, 5, 6.
Burja, A., 20, 21, 31, 46, 49.
Bus, A. J. M., 92.
Büsch, J. G., 20, 21, 46.
Butte, W., 11.

Cajori, F., 24, 36, 48, 70.
calculus, differential and integral, 7, 15, 20, 21, 30, 40, 46, 47, 48ff., 61, 63, 64, 67, 68, *68—74*; Novalis' "fundamental formula of calculus," 72; *see also specific concepts*.
Cantor, M., 28, 29, 36, 49, 50.
Carlsson, A., 17.
Carlyle, Th., 1.
Cassirer, E., 14, 15.
categories, 14, 41, 79, mathematical c., 41, 62, dynamic c., 41, 62.
Cauchy, A. L., baron, 47.
Cayley, A., 55.
"characteristica generalis," 22, *58f*.
Charpentier, J. F. W. von, 35f., 37; Julie, 35f.
chemistry *or* alchemy & math., 12, 34, 36, 92.

Chladni, E. F. F., 87, 90, 91.
Die Christenheit oder Europa, 87.
circle, *60f.*, 86; squaring the c., 40, 60, 61, 78.
Cohen, H., 15.
Condillac, E. B. de, 24.
Condorcet, M. J. A. N. C., marquis de, 24.
conic sections, 60.
continuity, 15, 16, 74,
combinatorial analysis, 22, 28ff., 46, 59, 63, 67, 68, 86, 92; school of c.a., 28f., 64; *see also* "ars combinatoria."
counting, *64f.*
Courant, R., 20, 62.
Crelle, A. L., 21.

d'Alembert, J. le R., 39, 47, 57, 75.
definition, 16, 32, 52, *53-55*, 60, 87.
derivative, 47, 49; "fluxions," 47, 69, 70.
Descartes, R., 22, 44, 89, 90, 93.
dialectic math., 19, 30.
differential, 48ff., 68, 69; d. quotient, 50, 69, 70.
Dilthey, W., 4, 9, 10, 19.
Dirichlet, P. J. Lejeune, 89.
disease, 40.
dogma, 40, 63, 77, 80.
Dohmke, J., 6.
Dumas, C. G. F., 8, 56.

Eckartshausen, K. von, 13, 33, 45.
Eckhart, Meister, 2.
École Polytechnique, 20.
economics & math., 24.
ego *or* non-ego, 44, 45, 68, 80.
Eichner, H., 86.
Einstein, A., 15.
Eisenhart, L. R., 55.
electricity, 34, 93.
empirical, 39, 41, 67, 68, 76, 81.
encyclopedia, universal, 22, 34, 35, 75-77, 81, 87, 92; *Encyclopédie*, 45, 75.
enthusiasm & math., 45.
epic, 83.

equation, 26, 35, 64.
Eratosthenes, sieve of, 29.
ethics & math., 24, 32, 77.
Euclid, 26, 38, 54, 55, 59, 60, 90.
Euler, L., 20, 22, 23, 37, 42, 47, 50, 51, 53, 62, 70, 71, 72, 73.
existence, 52, 65.
extrasensory perception, 43.

Fauteck, H., 82.
Fichte, J. G., 32, 33, 38, 42, *44f.*, 58, 80.
finite; f. magnitude, 48, 66; calculus of f. differences, 49.
Fischer, E. G., 30f.
formalization of math., 71f.
Fourrier, J., 90.
fragments, 1, 17, 37, 94; f. as literary genre & math., 86.
Frederick the Great, 24.
free creation, math. *or* literature as, 13, 17, 23, 33, 40, 60, 65, 78, 81, 86f., *see also* "ars inveniendi."
freedom, 40, 41.
Freiberg, Mining Academy at, 21, 27, 31, 33f., 35, 37, 94.
Friedell, E., 11f.
Friedmann, H., 7.
function, 15, 16, 68, 69, 74; trigonometric f., 90.

Galvani, L., 34.
Gauss, K. F., 27, 31, 47, 89.
Gehler, J. S. T., 6, 8.
Gellert, C. F., 27.
genius & math., 40, 41, 44, 57.
geology, 34.
geometry, 7, 8, 22, 26, 32, 38, 43, 46, *58-61*, 62, 71, 73, 77, 88, 91; ancient g., 48; elementary vs. higher g., 59; g. & human mind, 58; mystical g., 16, 45; non-Euclidean, 15, 38, 55, 56; *see also specific concepts*.
God, 23, 40, 41, 42, 55, 68, 81.
Gode- von Aesch, A. von, 17, 18, 19, 25.

105

Goethe, J. W. von, 15, 18, 25, 27, 33, 39, 57, 59, 65, 94; *Wilhelm Meister*, 84.
Göttingen, University at, 20, 26.
grammar, 77, 79, 81, 82, 92.
Grandi, G., 23.
Gruson, J. P., 21.

Haering, Th., 18, 19, 30, 35, 38, 72, 75, 79.
Halle, 31.
Hamburger, K., preface, 9, 14-16, 17, 18, 19, 40, 50, 74, 79.
Hardenberg, Erasmus von (Novalis' brother), 32.
Hardenberg, Karl von (Novalis' brother), 46.
Hartmann, N., 79.
Hauff, J. K. F., 21, 46.
Haussmann, J. H., 9.
Havenstein, E., 12, 19, 67.
Haym, R., 10f., 19.
Hederer, E., 18, 19, 52.
Heilborn, E., 6, 10, 11, 19.
Helmholtz, H. L. F. von, 89, 90.
Helmstedt, University at, 26, 31.
Hemsterhuis, F., 6, 8, 33, 35, 38, 44, 45, 55, 56.
Herder, J. G. von, 25.
Heynitz, A. von, 34.
Hiebel, F., 18, 19, 36.
Hilbert, D., 60.
Hindenburg, K. F., 20, 21, 27ff., 37, 46, 64.
history, 35, 63, 93; h. of math., 20-25, 77.
Hofmann, J. E., 50.
Huch, R., 11.
Hugenstein, A. H. von, 6.
Hülsen, A. L., 38.
humanities, 26.
Husserl, E., 15.
"Hymnen an die Nacht," fifth, 89.
"hymns to math.," 4, 10, 11, 17, 19, 37, 92.

Iliad, 83.
Imle, F., 13.
immortality, 40, 41.
infinitesimal(s), 23, 48, 49, 50, 51, 70, 71, 72, 73; "vanishing quantities," 47.
infinity, 11, 15, 16, 21, 22, 46, 48, 50, 51, 69, 72, 73, 74, 86, 87; i. series *or* sequence, 7, 64, 65, 66, 68, 78, 84, 85, 86; convergent and divergent i.s., 66; *see also* infinitesimal(s), and progression.
intuition (Anschauung), 15, 41, 42, 77; a priori i., 44.
irrationalism, 33, 35.

Jani, D. C., 25.
Jena, University at, 21, 26.
Journal de l'École Polytechnique, 21.
Journal für reine und angewandte Mathematik, 21.
judgment; a priori j., 39; analytic j., 39; empirical j., 39; synthetic j., 39; How are a priori synthetic judgments possible?, 39, 40, 44.
Just, A. C., 31, 37.

Kamnitzer, E., 7.
Kant, I., 10, 12, 14, 26, 31, 33, *38-44*, 57, 62, 63, 73, 80, 81, 93.
Kästner, A. G., 20, 25, 27f., 46, 47, 48, 49, 50.
Kepler, J., 90.
Kerékjártó, B. von, 62.
Kleeberg, L., 13.
Kleist, H. von, 16, 91.
Kline, M., 10, 23, 90, 91.
Kluckhohn, P. 3, 5, 17, 19, 25, 67, 85.
Klügel, G. S., 50, 64.
knowledge, 42, 43, 57, 62, 87; a priori k., 43f., 81; extrasensory k., 43; science of k., 45, 58.
known & unknown, 66, 85.
Kronecker, L., 87.
Kühn, Sophie von, 4, 5, 32ff., 94.

The Ladies Diary..., 21.
Lagrange, J. L., 20, 21, 22, 46, 47, 67.
L'Hospital, G. F. A. de, 47.
language & math., 6, 16, 61, *81f.*, 89;
  l. as "Gedankenmeter," 76, 82; l. &
  life, 89; l. like math. formulae, 81;
  object & syntax l. in math., 52f.
La Mettrie, J. O. de, 24.
Laplace, P. S., marquis de, 20, 21, 46.
Lavoisier, A. L., 34.
law, 26.
Die Lehrlinge zu Sais, 87, 88, 92.
Leibniz, G. W. von, 15, 22, 23, 28, 39,
  40, 47, 48, 50, 57, 59, 69, 70, 89, 90,
  91, 92, 93.
Leipzig, University at, 21, 26, 27f.,
  37, 94.
Leipziger Magazin für reine und angewandte Mathematik, 21.
Lempe, J. F., 36.
Lichtenberg, G. C., 25.
life & math., 24, 46, 58, 60, 61, 89;
  l. & death, 94; elixir of l. & math.,
  61.
Lindemann, F. von, 61.
line, straight, 48, 55, *60*; skew l., 48, *60*.
limit, 47, 66, 73, 84.
Linnaeus (Karl von Linne), 59.
literature, 16, 35, 62, 63, 65, 74, *83-89*;
  see also epic, fragment, novel, poetry,
  Romanticism, *and individual works
  of Novalis.*
Lobachevsky, N.I., 55.
Lobkowitz, C. de, 24.
logarithms, 26, 46, 74, 76, 82, 85.
logic, 35, 52, 76, 81, 82, 92.
Lorey, W., 21, 27.
Locher-Ernst, L., 17, 90.
Lull, Ramon, 28.

magic, 11, 13, 14, 17, 21, 40, 41, 89,
  93; m. & math., 34, *79f.*, m. idealism,
  12; m. i. & definition, 54, 79f., m. is
  genuine math., 80.

magnitude, 7, 42, 48, 62, *65f.*, 70, 71,
  73, 81.
Mahnke, D., 16, 61.
Malfatti, G., 11.
Mann, Th., *Der Zauberberg*, 83.
mathematical texts, 46.
mathematical training, 25ff., 37, 46,
  94.
"mathesis universalis," 22, 93.
mathematics, math. of math., 77; see
  Table of Contents *and specific terms
  and concepts.*
matter, 58; m. & form, 78.
Maupertuis, P. M. L. de, 24.
mechanics & math., 58, 77.
medicine & math., 24, 34.
Meissner, C., 6.
"Messkunst," 87f.
metaphor, mathematical, 82.
metaphysics & math., 8, 24, 39, 61.
method, mathematical, 15, 44, 52, 53,
  60, 69, 73, 76, 77, 78, 82; m. &
  madness, 40, 68; scientific m., 53;
  statistical m., 67.
Merriman, G. M., 61.
Michelsen, J. A. C., 50, 70, 71, 72, 73.
mineralogy, 34.
mining engineering, 34.
Minor, J., 5, 6, 7.
modality & math., 41, 45, 62.
Mollweide, K. B., 27.
Mönch, K., 50.
Montucla, J. F., 23f.
Mozart, W. A., 89.
Müller, A., 9.
Müller, M., 42.
music & math., 13, 16, 17, 18, 34,
  43, 58, 61, 65, *89-92*, 93, 94; m. & algebra, 92; m. & calculus, 91; m. &
  nature, 91; m. & universe, 91; "m.
  is an arithmetic exercise of the soul,"
  90, 91; fugue, 92.
mysticism & math., 16, 17, 21, 33, 45,
  48, 53, 61, 64, 65, 69, 85.

107

Napier, W. F. P., 82.
Natorp, P., 15.
nature & math., 6, 77, 87, 93; *see also* universe.
Neo-Kantian School, 16.
Newton, I., 22, 23, 50, 69.
novel, 83, 84, 85.
number, 6, 11, 23, 61, 62, *64f.*, 82, 88, 89, 91, 92.

object, objective, 15, 68, 76.
Heinrich von Ofterdingen, 63, 87, 88.
Olshausen, W., 10, 19, 27, 28, 31.
one, 11, 23.
operations, basic, *66-68*, 77, 79, 81.
optics & math., 77.
oryctognosy & math., 59.

Pascal, B., 22, 32, 33, 45.
perpetual motion, 40, 41.
perspective & math., 77.
Pfaff, J. F., 31.
philosopher's stone, 61, 78.
philosophy & math., 7, 11, 18, 21, 22, 26, 32, 33, *37-45*, 61, 63, 68, 74, 77, 77-79.
physics, 12, 34, 39, 63, 78; ph. & math., 8, 18, 77, 79, 93.
plane, 60.
plastic arts & math., 58.
Plato, 17.
Plotinus, 17, 33, 38.
Pitcairn, A., 24.
poetry *or* poetic, 13, 34, 40, 45, 92, 93, 94; p. & math., 48, 61, 63, 65, 68, 69, 77, 84, 87, 88; poet-priest-musician-magician-mathematician, 87, 94; "poeta philosophus," 87; "Universalpoesie," 84.
point, 54, *59f.*, 74.
"Potenz," 18, 85, 86; "Potenzreihe,' 85; "qualitative Potenzierung,' 85.
Priestley, J., 34.
principle of identity, 44; of contradiction, 44, 94; of sufficient reason 44.

progression, "Reihe," 7, 83, 84, 85, 86; arithmetic p., 83; geometric p., 83; p. as "Werden," 85; *see also* infinite series, sequence.
proof, 16, 52, *57f.*, circular p., 57f.
pure mathematics, preface, 15, 39, 42, 43, 61, 62, 63, 66, 77, 81.
Pythagoras *or* Pythagorean, 11, 17, 45, 57, 87, 90, 91, 92.

quadrivium of the *artes liberales*, 91.
quality, 36, 41, 42, 45, 62.
quantity, 36, 41, 42, 45, 62, 65, 66.
Quesnay, F., 24.

Rand, B., 40.
rationalism *or* reason, 14, 16, 24f., 39, 41, 61, 63, 76, 89; antinomies of pure reason, 57f.
Rehbein, J. H. E., 20, 21, 46.
Reinhold, K. L., 26, 31.
relation, 35, 41, 45, 62.
relativity, theory of, preface, 15f., 79.
religion & math., 16, 17, 23, 24, 32, 33, 34, 77, *80f.*, 93, 94; "sacra mathesis," 24; *see also* God.
rhythm & math., 13.
Ritter, J. W., 38.
Romanticism *or* Romantic, 11, 12, 15, 16, 17, 25, 47, 48, 83, 85, 91; r. vs. classical literature, 86; definitions of early German Romanticism, 86; „Romantisieren" & math., 12, 85; r. & algebra, 86; r. & combinatorial analysis, 86.
Rosenbloom, P., 52.
Russell, B., 15.

"sacra mathesis," 24.
Samuel, R., 3, 5, 8, 17, 19.
science & math., 17, 26, 33, 40, 55, 58, 61, 63, 68, 75, 76, 80, concrete sc.s, 79; healing power of sc., 32; total *or* universal sc., 33, 34, 35, 63, 78, 81.

"scientia generalis," 22.
Schelling, F. W. J. von, 35.
Schiller, J. C. F., 26.
Schlegel, F., 3, 4, 5, 31, 38, 48, 83, 84, 85, 86, 91; A. W., 35. 83.
Schmid, J. J., 24.
Schocken, S., 9.
Schulz, J., 50.
Seelig, C., 7.
semantics & calculus, 71.
Silz, W., 16, 91.
similarities & dissimilarities & math., 65, 76.
Simon, H., 12, 40, 79.
Smith, N. K., 42.
space, 15f., 38, 42, 43.
Speiser, A., 90, 91, 92.
Spenlé, E., 12.
sphere, 16, 17, 45; harmony of the sph.s, 87, 91.
Spiess, O., 23.
Spinoza, B. de, 32, 38, 44, 45.
spiral, 23.
spiritual & physical, 80, 87.
Stahl, K. D. M., 46, 50.
Strich, F., 91.
Struik, D. J., 21, 22, 23, 36, 47.
subject, subjective, 15, 68.
Sylvester, J. J., 89.
symbolism, 14, 52, 81, 82, 83, 86, 87, 89, 93; s. & math., 24, 28, 64, 65, 88; image, 88, 89.
synthesis *or* synthetic, 39, 40, 57, 78; absolute s., 93; s. & math., 13, 67, 68.

tautology & math., 57.
Taylor series, 47.
technology, 34, 94.
theorem, 7, 16, 32, 52, 54, *57*; binomial th., 29, 46, 57, 64; synthetic th., 57; tautological th., 57; Pythagorean th., 57.
thesis, antithesis, synthesis, 30.
thinking & math., 57, 76.
Tieck, L., 2, 3, 4, 5, 37, 63.
time, 15f., 38, 42, 43, 65.
Timerding, H. E., 24.
Töpfer, H. A., 20, 31, 46.
topology, 62.
truth, 1; t. & math., 38, 56; t. & falsity, 79.

universe, 35, 46, 65, 77, 80; u. & math., 14, 93; center of the u., 16, 17.

Vega, G. von, 46.
Vieth, G. U. A., 50.

Wagner, E. L., 17, 19, 34.
Walther, J., 27.
Walzel, O., 6.
Wasmuth, E., 7, 18.
Watson, J., 40.
Weissenfels, 37.
"Wenn nicht mehr Zahlen und Figuren," 62f., 88.
Werner, A. G., 34, 35, 38.
Wittenberg, University at, 21, 31.

zero, 11, 22, 23, 50, 51, 70, 71, 72, 73.